D1624114

Globalism: America's Demise

William Bowen, Jr.

Copyright © 1984 by William Bowen, Jr.
ISBN Number 0-910311-12-9
Library of Congress Catalog Card 84-080408
Printed in the United States of America

All rights reserved. No part of this book may be reproduced without permission from the publisher, except by a reviewer who may quote brief passages
in a review; nor may any part of this book be reproduced, stored in a retrieval
system or copied by mechanical, photocopying, recording or other means,
without permission from the publisher.

Cover art by R. Mark Heath, cover graphics by Lloyd M. Marcus, and inside
book illustrations by Larry Miner.

Dedication

Penny and I are dedicating this book to Jason and Steve Bowen, our two sons, and to Stephen Guertler, "whose boss is a Jewish carpenter." Jason and Steve are still too young to understand the battle. Stephen Guertler is already in training to become a lieutenant in the Lord's army.

It is Christian youth who must be prepared to take up the battle against Satan and the *new age* he plans to usher in. Our lack of vigilance and conviction hasn't preserved much of the inheritance rightfully due our Christian youth. We have lost much of it to the master of deception. Sadly, we will lose more before the victory is won, but God will prevail.

The inheritance we can win back, but who will win the children? To save them we will be persecuted, but we must stand firm. Compromise is a victory for the enemy.

The time is now for all to decide whether they are on the Lord's side — or Satan's.

Table of Contents

Foreword

We are living in urgent, critical times of great opportunity for Believers! We are encompassed about by the enemy with the world looking on. What a marvelous time in which the power of the Lord can be revealed to them through us.

Imagine the amazement and joy when the lost and despairing world sees all our infirmities and imperfections overcome and used to accomplish victories for God's glory. Isn't it exciting to know that our generation has been honored by God as the messengers of salvation. Hallelujah!

What's the enemy's game plan? Read this book.

Introduction

The purpose of this remarkable book by William Bowen, Jr., is quite clear: Rather than lecture a world awash in negatives and hopelessness, Bill Bowen chooses to remind us of the beauty, the hope and the salvation of John 3:16. The remedy for the critical problems facing our nation is there for all to see. The question is whether we have the faith to do it.

To *solve* a problem we must first *understand* it. And to understand it, we must open our eyes and ears and hearts to the fact that the problem exists, and that it is gnawing at all we hold precious.

Bill and Penny Bowen are an inspiring Christian couple who have dedicated their lives to helping educate the body of Christ. True enough, they dare to ask questions that are obliged to be asked: Are we willing to *act* at all costs? Are we part of the solution — or merely part of the problem? Are we willing to accept the mandate of James 1:22, and become doers of the word, and not hearers only? Do we accept the admonition of James 2:26 that faith without works is dead?

The *Globalism* of which Bill Bowen warns is not some abstract contrivance of rhetoric. It is real, and it is rapidly growing and expanding under the mesmerizing auspices and direction of politicians and religionists. But as Bill Bowen makes clear, both *Globalism* and humanism can, and must, be countered by a genuine return to American patriotism and principles, and by the joining together of Christians in a moral revival across our land and thence around the world.

Read this book carefully, and ponder it prayerfully. It is a powerful message of hope and joy — and salvation.

Jesse Helms, Senator
United States Senate

CHAPTER 1

Globalism: A Bottom Line

Have I not commanded you? Be strong and courageous!
Do not tremble or be dismayed, for the Lord your
God is with you wherever you go.
Joshua 1:9

We Christians, this country and our families we love so much are not meant to survive the 1980s — physically or ideologically.

The globalists — an astute generation of internationalists — have targeted these three groups for elimination. The reason? Because these three entities stand in the way of the completion of an economic, political and social network which will be global in scope.

This global plan has been developed over a long period of time and should not be underestimated. The globalists are intelligent and possess intense zeal for their cause. They also wield almost limitless power because of their wealth and position.

The globalists are convinced that what they are doing is for the eventual salvation of mankind and the planet earth. The greatest strength they possess is that the general public in this land does not even know that they exist.

My people are destroyed for lack of knowledge.
Hosea 4:6

The objective of this global initiative is *control*. Although the desire to rule the world is not a new ambition, the control sought by this present generation of global imperialists is more than government, wealth and resources. They control these already. What the globalists want in order to complete their plan is control of population.

Their objective of global control is simple, but its implementation is complex and convoluted. It is mind-boggling when one attempts to unravel it — truly a tangled web of deception. Their control of population is in their ability to manage the thoughts and behavior of the masses: the key being *consensus*; the motivation, *survival*.

If the struggle were a physical one, we could identify our enemy more readily and recognize the dangers coming against us. Like the serpent in the garden, the sophistication and refinement of the psychological weaponry are so subtle that we are now in the final stages of the conflict with only a few awakening to the conflict's existence.

As a measure of the effectiveness of these new techniques we need only recall the unfenced concentration camps during the Korean and Vietnam conflicts. Due to psychological intimidation the captured American military did not try to escape. The same behavioral control exists today, but everyone is a prisoner, the earth is the concentration camp and the globalists are the stalag commandants.

The family is not meant to survive the 1980s.

For our struggle is not against flesh and blood . . .
Ephesians 6:12

In the past we Christians have always been too late with too little. We cannot afford that mistake this time. If Christians want to preserve their right to live and worship freely and Americans want to retain a national identity, we must stop indulging ourselves in the luxury of fighting each other and direct our energies against the enemy.

There is much to be done and very little time in which to do it. If this nation falls, and its end is very near, there is no place else to go.

In-fighting has dissipated our energies and brought us to our present calamitous condition — yet the dissension continues. We are now at a point where we must decide if we are going to be on the Lord's side or continue doing it our way which will lead to ultimate disaster.

Why the Family?

"The American family structure produces mentally ill children."
— Ashley Montagu, Lecture at Anaheim, California, to 1000 home economic teachers, 9 November 1970. (See also, *Humanistic Morals and Values Education*, Vince Nesbitt, N.S.W. 2066 Australia, p.5).

There are many ministries, both religious and secular, being created to "solve" the problems of the American family. Unfortunately these ministries are committed to symptomatic treatment, but none have discerned the basic cause that brought about the problems.

Granted, the ultimate cause is sin, but the advocates of globalism, as we will see, are even trying to corner that market. The disintegration of the American family has not just happened; it is an important part of the global program.

Children are imprinted at a very young age with parent-transferred values such as belief in God and patriotism. If these beliefs are obstacles to the creation of a global network of control, then it becomes essential for the globalists to eliminate the family influence at the earliest possible age.

In the past and continuing today the erasing of parental imprinting has been done by alienating the child and parent. The recently created generation gap is an example. However, in the near future we will see strategies designed to remove the child physically from the presence of the parents.

It doesn't take much effort to catalogue methods already in vogue for achieving this end, ranging from advertising that fosters a standard of living which keeps both parents employed and out of the home to frivolous definitions of child abuse to justify the state's removal of the child from the home. (Child abuse and child neglect laws, because they are undefined, are the greatest danger to the family and the most powerful laws in existence).

A skilled observer will soon discover that public education policy is a major perpetrator in pitting child and parent against one another, and the community school program in which the child lives at the school will complete the termination of parental rights to any say in the raising of our children.

How to get what YOU want?

Globalism, humanism, socialism, feminism, illuminism, New Age, etc. are all the same animal: the differences are semantic and inconsequential.

Humanism argues paradoxically that Man is philosophically more important than any god, yet in its implementation the individual life has very little value. Man is but a throw away in today's humanistic society.

"The world has cancer and the cancer is Man," observed one globalist in the book, *Mankind at a Turning Point.*

Suicide, euthanasia, abortion, even homosexual marriages are all extermination procedures. All are accepted practices in the isms mentioned above. All are atheistic; all are given to one-world government; and all hold human life in very low regard.

Not only the novice but on occasion the veteran investigator will fail to remember that control is the bottom line in this immense and very intricate maze. Contradiction or paradox are merely philosophical considerations of no importance to the manipulators. As a result the decision makers pulling the crisis management/behavior modification strings support both sides of an issue to create conflict which forces resolution which brings change.

Change is necessary to keep society moving toward the ultimate globalist goal — total global control. Conflict evolves from opposing points of view, and if none exists, it is easy to create.

To the globalists there is no inconsistency in proclaiming the importance of human rights while instigating the annihilation of millions. There is no conflict of interest in funding both the KKK and the NAACP. There is no incompatibility in pumping billions of dollars into the communist and socialist economies while serving as leaders of the Free World. There is no duplicity in controlling the National Education Association (NEA) and creating the Progressive Education Association (PEA) to represent an opposing point of view.

The Formula

First, create a problem — real or imaginary.

Second, advertise the problem — convince people that something must be done.

Third, provide your solution.

Result: change brought about so things are YOUR way.

For example: infrequently high school girls become pregnant. The proponents of sex education begin publicizing these occurrences to such an extent that the public is convinced something must be done to prevent the "collapse" of society. The advertisers of the problem are happy to offer their solution which is sex education.

To get the nose of the camel in the tent the instruction would be entirely voluntary, for seniors only, for a half hour once a week. Boys and girls would be taught separately and all aspects of the program would be monitored and approved by the parents and community being served. Does that sound like the sex-ed program we have today?

Now that we have the whole beast in the tent, sex-ed is mandated kindergarten through twelfth grades; the classes are co-ed; masturbation for both sexes, fantasizing, diverse lifestyles and other perversions are encouraged for experimentation; and parents and the community are intruders.

Abortion counseling is commonplace and school time is frequently used for pupils to have abortions without the knowledge or consent of parents. Pregnancy among school children has become epidemic and reaches into the earliest possible age. Teenagers, desensitized by sex-ed instruction, become adults who swell porno parlors and abortion clinics, which are the major funders of sex-ed promotion when federal funding isn't forthcoming. Proceeds from such enterprises mushroom into billions of dollars each year, spilling over into the even more lucrative drug scene. On and on the ripple effect of change goes, bringing into being a greater infusion of humanistic/globalist programming.

The current conflict-resolution-change program is child and sexual abuse. This program is now very heavily into the advertising stage. In this case, although the incidence of child and sexual abuse has not increased significantly, the broader or more liberal interpretation of these terms to include spanking as child abuse and tickling as a sex abuse has had the effect of making it appear that society is being inundated by these problems.

The jingo press readily provides all the publicity needed and programmed social workers and teachers do the rest. The desired change is the termination of parental rights. The government will then raise the children free from parental imprinting about God and nation. Remember, it was Hitler who rightly said that they who control the youth control the future.

Why must God go?

> "Any child who believes in God is mentally ill." — Paul Brandwein, *The Social Sciences,* p. T 10, Harcourt Brace, 1970. (See also Nesbitt, p. 5).

In the New Age of Globalism belief in God is a sin, patriotism is irrelevant and family is archaic. The state replaces these: Caesar becomes god, planetary citizenship becomes the mark for survival and government becomes the family.

As defined in volume two of *Global 2000 Report to the President* (1980), globalism rests on the Malthusian theory that the world's resources are going to be exhausted, that replacement resources are not going to be forthcoming and that the world's population must be brought in line with what the world's *present* resources can sustain.

The globalists estimate that the world can only sustain a 2.5-billion population by the year 2000, but "Spaceship Earth" already has in excess of 4.5-billion people. The Global 2000 hypothesis makes it essential for the globalists not only to bring population growth to a stand still, but it also becomes necessary for a roll back in population; hence, zero population programs.

There is a way which seems right to a man, but its end is

the way of death.
                    Proverbs 14:12

Population roll back can be accomplished in a number of ways such as revolutions — especially when communist victories result in the extermination of millions of dissidents (don't forget that Christians will be dissidents in the New Age) — and famine.

Famine can be a programmed result as well as the result of a natural catastrophe. Farming has always been a debtor economy and with the Federal Reserve maintaining high interest rates banks are becoming the new owners of more farm operations than bonafide farmers. (The Federal Reserve is a *non*-governmental agency controlled by the globalist international bankers — accountable to no one and totally unsupervised).

Other population control methods would be suicide, euthanasia, homosexuality, sterilization and abortion. Homosexuality is on the rise, encouraged by the sex-ed program in the schools. Euthanasia bills are introduced every year in state legislatures. Suicide is the number-two killer of school-age youth. Abortion is now 1.5 million per year — and growing! (Abortion is big business when you multiply 1.5 million times the cost of even the cheapest abortion). To a Christian, these practices are immoral and unacceptable even though some of them have been legalized. Therefore, the globalists say the Christian and his morality must be eradicated. In a godless or values-free society anything legal then becomes right and unchallenged.

Why the U.S.A.?

"Every child in America who enters school at the age of five is mentally ill, because he comes to school with allegiance toward our elected officials, toward our founding fathers, toward our institutions, toward the preservation of this form of government .."

patriotism, nationalism, sovereignty ... All of that proves the children are sick, because the truly well individual is one who has rejected all of those things and is what I would call the true international child of the future."
— Dr. Pierce of Harvard University, addressing 2000 teachers in Denver, Colorado, 1973. See "Education to Remold the Child," *Parent and Child Advocates*, Rt. 4, Watertown, Wisconsin 53094, U.S.A., p. 30. (See also Nesbitt, p.5).

As the late planetary citizen and designer of the geodesic dome "Bucky" Fuller said, "Nationalism is the blood clot in the world's circulatory system."
It is self-evident why patriotism or loyalty to a nation would be a stumbling block to the creation of a global government. Russian nationalism is just as evident as patriotism in the United States. Eventually Russian nationalism will have to go but that nation is already socialistic and atheistic.
The United States is under greater attack by the globalists because it still holds to a belief in God, possesses a remnant of the free enterprise system and is nationalistic. The Russians only have one strike against them, whereas we have three.

The globalists are formidable adversaries. They pursue their goals with a zeal and determination to be envied by the best of Christian evangelists. They are veterans, seasoned in their conviction that what they are doing is for the welfare of all mankind.
Their immense success in amassing power into their own hands fans their belief that they are right into a ruthless fanaticism. Ironically, despite all their writings, conventions and speeches in which they openly express their goals and intentions, it is our ignorance that they even exist that grants them immunity.

I urge people who disbelieve what I am saying to look into these matters for themselves and not just brush them aside. They will discover all that they have been told is true — and much more. In trying to prove me wrong, be prepared for a shocking discovery.

CHAPTER 2

Humanism:
The Abomination of Desolation

Your sons and your daughters shall be given to another people, while your eyes shall look on and yearn for them continually; but there shall be nothing you can do ... Because you did not serve the Lord your God...
Deuteronomy 28:31,47

"It's OK to lie ...
"It's OK to steal ...
"It's OK to have pre-marital sex ...
"It's OK to cheat ...
"It's OK to kill — if these things are part of your own value system and you have clarified these values for yourself."
— Dr. Murray Norris, *Weep for Your Children*
Box 73, Clovis, CA 93613, p. 6.

The quotation from Dr. Norris' book is an explanation by Erica Carle of Sidney Simon's values clarification. Dr.

Simon's courses are very popular in educational circles across the nation. In many areas his courses are required for teacher certification. A great deal has been written about Dr. Simon's values clarification and the associated strategies.

Such values are taught to our children beginning in kindergarten (even preschool day care centers use *T. A. for Tots*) and through the twelfth grades by the public schools as well as many private and church schools. Unfortunately the federal government funds many of the humanist programs which propagate these values.

The teaching of Dr. Simon's values clarification has resulted in a curious dichotomy. Among educationists the Simon methodologies are strongly defended but from among the parents a mounting wave of sharp criticism is rising.

The real question now is to whom do the children belong — the parent or the public schools, i.e., the state? Where does the final say belong as to what can be done to and with public school children? As more and more parents are discovering — usually too late — the humanist courts are deciding in favor of the state!

Too large a segment of the general public takes the stance that these educational issues are of no concern to them. Either they have no children, their children are no longer of school age or their children are safely in a private or church school. *THERE ARE NO OUTSIDERS IN PUBLIC EDUCATION.* Everyone is paying the bill for this excessively expensive public disgrace.

Education budgets are greatly overfunded by politicians intimidated by the education lobby, the largest and most powerful special interest group in the world. Public education is a terrible waste of tax money. Private and church schools that follow traditional academic standards do a superior job for one-third the cost of public education. It does not take a lot of time and money to educate children. It does take a lot of time and money to indoctrinate and modify their values.

Not only are you paying the bill for secular education, but you are to be the victim.

It is well to remember that those innocent, pink-cheeked little dears filling the playgrounds are going to be the globalist/humanist- programmed leaders of the future. Whether they are our children, it is of concern to everyone what the public schools are teaching.

As tedious as it can be, the general public must begin scrutinizing and challenging educational materials and curricula. We already have two humanized and Simonized generations, because we failed to be vigilant and allowed ourselves to be deceived by the educrats.

What misleads or deceives the public most often are the innocent titles of various educational programs — educational doublespeak. Beware of all programs concerning values and morals in the public schools. Values education in the public schools is based on Dr. Simon's no-values system, i.e., no right and no wrong. Morals education in the public schools is based on Lawrence Kohlberg's religious humanism, which is atheistic and man-centered.

For the sake of clarity it is worth the time and space to determine what humanism is. In 1933 and again in 1973 *Humanist Manifestos* were published so the world would know what humanists believed. These complete documents are in the Appendix, but some passages must be highlighted.

"First ... We believe ... that traditional dogmatic or authoritarian religions that place revelation, God, ritual, or creed above human needs and experience do a disservice to the human species ... As non-theists, we begin with humans not God, nature not deity ... No deity will save us; we must save ourselves ...

"Third: We affirm that moral values derive their source from human experience. Ethics is autonomous and *situational,* needing no theological or ideological sanctions . . . We strive for the good life, here and now . . .

"Fifth . . . Although science can account for the causes of behavior, the possibilities of individual *freedom of choice* exist in human life and should be increased.

"Sixth: In the area of sexuality, we believe that intolerant attitudes . . . unduly repress sexual conduct. The right to *birth control, abortion,* and *divorce* should be recognized . . . individuals should be permitted to express their sexual proclivities and pursue their life-styles as they desire.

"Seventh . . . a full range of civil liberties . . . includes a recognition of an individual's right to die with dignity, euthanasia, and the right to suicide.

"Eighth . . . We extend participatory democracy to . . . the family . . . People are more important than decalogues, rules, proscriptions, or regulations. (The Decalogue is the Ten Commandments).

"Ninth: *The separation of church and state and the separation of ideology and state are imperatives* . . .

"Twelfth: We deplore the division of humankind on nationalistic grounds. We have reached a turning point in human history where the best option is to transcend the limits of national sovereignty and to move toward the *building of a world community* . . . We look to the development of a system of *world law* and a *world order* based upon transnational federal government."

See to it that no one takes you captive through philosophy and empty deception, according to the tradition of men, according to the elementary

principles of the world, rather than according to Christ.
Colossians 2:8

The semantic confusion that exists about humanism and humanists is understandable and planned.

A principal in a senior high school in Harford County, Maryland, was quoted in the local press as saying, "I am a humanist — but I don't know what that is."

This mentality is typical of middle management in the public school system, but unwittingly the principal is right in both instances: he is a humanist but doesn't know what one is. Many confuse humanism with the term humane, and humanist with humanitarian. Beneath the smoke screen of high-sounding phrases and platitudes is a demonic philosophy committed to a one-world or globalist government, the enslavement of man and the eradication of God, nation and family.

In his closing remarks to the *Humanist Manifesto II,* the author, Paul Kurtz, correctly observed, "The true *revolution* is occurring and can continue in countless non-violent *adjustments.*" Conflict (revolution), resolution (adjustment) and change: the globalist/socialist/humanist formula for change.

The *Humanist Manifesto I* confirms in its opening remarks that it is establishing a new religion. Although present-day humanists deny humanism is a religion, much of the *Humanist Manifesto II* is devoted to religious matters. The United States Supreme Court cited humanism as a religion in the 1961 case of *Torcaso v. Watkins* (367 U. S. 488).

Based on this decision, Rep. John B. Conlan's 1976 amendment to the Higher Education Act (H. R. 12851/S. 2657) confirmed humanism to be a religion and declared it unconstitutional to teach humanism in the public schools. The amendment also prohibited the use of federal funds to support educational projects or programs involving humanism. Although Christianity was quickly removed from the public schools, obviously the same has not been true of humanism.

What is shocking is the extent to which humanism has displaced Christianity in our nation. Almost every humanist doctrine quoted from the manifesto is in evidence in our courts, our federal, state and local legislation, and in our society and schools.

Abraham Lincoln was quite correct in pointing out that the educational philosophy of today becomes the political policy of tomorrow.

The United States Supreme Court has legalized abortion, birth control is commonly practiced, divorce has reached the 50-percent mark, gay rights and child rights are vigorously pushed, suicide and infanticide are commonplace, laws are broken with immunity, morality is violated publicly and on and on the catalogue continues.

Although the separation of church and state is not found anywhere in the Constitution, including the first amendment, the Supreme Court chose to follow the *Humanist Manifesto* rather than the Constitution and decided in favor of the separation of church and state.

Congress shall make no law respecting an establishment of religion, or prohibiting the free exercise thereof; or abridging the freedom of speech, or of the press; or the right of the people peaceably to assemble, and to petition the government for a redress of grievances.
            Article I to the Constitution (1791)

The teaching of American history and government has been under attack for so long and corrupted by so many "innovative ideas" that the American public is ignorant of the fact that the Constitution was written to protect the people. The Constitution does not give any rights to the people. Its purpose is to protect the rights of the people and give only those rights to the government that the people want the government to have. A federal republic, not a democracy, was established. In a constitutional republic the highest office is *citizen*

A threat to the parent and the family exists in the present push by the Social Services to create participatory democracy in the family. This seemingly innocent-sounding term means that everyone in the family has a vote. There is no authority figure such as the father or the mother in the father's absence.

This is one of the covert reasons for the push for Kiddie Lib and Child's Rights. (A rule of thumb worth remembering is to look for *both* the *overt* and *covert* objectives behind any UNESCO or Social Services push, e.g., International Year of the Woman).

If children's rights are enlarged then parental rights are reduced proportionately. With such counseling and indoctrination it becomes increasingly clear why children are disobedient and rebellious. School counselors — who want to justify their existence and be needed — relentlessly pit child against parent.

Family dissension between parent and child has been programmed and often encouraged by unwitting bleeding-heart teachers and social workers who themselves compensate for their own deficiencies by playing the role of a surrogate parent to our children.

Parents, unaware of this subversion or its source, throw up their hands in despair over their inability to control their children and abdicate their right to run their own homes. The children then control the home and reduce it to anarchy as would be expected with immature mentalities in control; a perfect excuse for the state's enlarging its participation in the family.

The purpose or covert objective of PET or Parent Effectiveness Training isn't to put the parent back in control of the child but to get the parent to *relate,* which translates into acceptance of the child's willfulness. The conflict is

resolved not by getting the child to submit to the paren·
but by CHANGING THE PARENT'S VALUES to be the
same as the values (or non-values) taught the children in
the public schools; hence, compatibility.

A Department of Human Resources advertisement
appeared on a major Baltimore television station during
the summer of 1982 with a small girl crying and saying,
"My mother called me dumb and that hurt my feelings
and my daddy spanked me and said it hurt him more than
it did me."
An adult voice then came on advising the listening
children that if this happened to them they should call the
two toll-free numbers pictured on the screen and report
their parents for child abuse.

*They will be divided, father against son, and son against
father, mother against daughter, and daughter against
mother . . .*
Luke 12:53

Americans are haunted by the feeling that something is
wrong in the land but find it difficult to decide what it is
and who is responsible. Even more frightening is the realization that one is helpless against these unseen, unidentified forces that have robbed the people of the Great
American Dream without putting something optimistic
and inspiring in its place. Instead, pessimism, a sense of
helplessness and *despair* (Lawrence Kohlberg's sixth
stage of moral reasoning) are all pervasive.
People in despair are easily controlled. The globalists
know this and have programmed this behavior so they
can control the people.

How can an entire nation be programmed?

Every public school system in the United States and

most private and church schools are based on the "progressive education" philosophy of John Dewey. Check the signers of the *Humanist Manifesto I* and in addition to the name of Mondale you find John Dewey's. Public education with its compulsory attendance "victims" was the vehicle to infuse humanist, no-god theology into every area of American society.

John Dewey's progressive education is the *Humanist Manifesto I*. Sidney Simon's values clarification and Lawrence Kohlberg's moral reasoning are *Humanist Manifestos I and II*.

Is humanism and "progressive education" really any threat to the American system?

1) The Marxist Connection
"Humanism is the denial of God and the total affirmation of man . . . Humanism is really nothing else but Marxism."
— *Karl Marx, Economic Politique et Philsophie*

2) The Soviet Connection
"Soviet society today is the real embodiment of the ideas of proletarian, socialist humanism."
— Leonid Brezhnev, "On the Policy of the Soviet Union and The International Situation," Novosti Press Agency Publishing House, Moscow – Doubleday & Co., Inc., Garden City, NY, 1973, p.27.

3) The Feminist-Gay Rights Connection
a. "It is absurd to say . . . that one is a humanist but not a feminist . . . feminism is the last evolutionary development of humanism. Feminism is humanism on its most advanced level."
— Riane Eisler, *Humanist Magazine* (November/December, 1980). Riane Eisler wrote *The Equal Rights (ERA) Handbook*.

b. *"Feminism is the path to humanism, and it is humanism that is the goal."*
— Gloria Steinam, Nevada State Women's Conference, *The Humanist,* (November/December, 1977). The theme of the 1978 American Humanist Association was "Humanism and Feminism." Gloria Steinam is a feminist author and leader.

c. "Overthrowing capitalism is too small for us. We must overthrow the whole f_____ patriarchy!"
— Gloria Steinam, Michigan Free Press, (April 15, 1974).

d. "By the year 2000 we will . . . raise our children to believe in human potential, not God."
— Gloria Steinam, *Saturday Review of Education,* March 1973; See also Norris, p. 22).

e. "School counselors should be required to take courses in which . . . a positive view of lesbianism is presented . . . students . . . encouraged to explore alternate lifestyles, including lesbianism . . . Schools (should) set up lesbian studies . . . use of lesbian books encouraged. . . Lesbian clubs should be set up in schools . . ."
— Jean O'Leary, co-executive director of the National Gay Task Force and an avowed lesbian. "Struggle to End Sex Bias in the Public Schools," New York Chapter of NOW. See *Christian Be Watchful,* Texas Eagle Forum, 1978-1980, pp. 12-13.

f. "This (feminism) is the first federally-funded revolution."
— Mildred Persinger, United Nations representative of the national board, YWCA of the U.S.A., at the opening session of the Colorado IWY conference. See *Christian Be Watchful,* 1980, p. 13.

Obviously feminism is not equal pay for equal work and humanism and socialism are not alien philosophies. Although educationists make up a large part of the signers of the *Humanist Manifestos,* leaders in theology, the arts, entertainment and the feminist movement — all of the antibiblical movements of today — are represented.

Many school administrators and educationists will argue that humanism and values clarification do not exist in their schools or systems. Unfortunately such disclaimers are not true, although the person making the disclaimer may honestly believe that he is stating the truth.

Every public school regardless of the grade level is evaluated every ten years. The evaluation is a long, exhaustive study that delves into every imaginable aspect of the school, its staff and its student body. Nothing goes unnoticed and the cost to the school and system is about $6,000 to $8,000 for each evaluated school, a terrible waste of money.

The guidelines for conducting the evaluation are included in a hefty volume entitled *Evaluative Criteria* and issued by the National Study of School Evaluation, a nonprofit corporate body that was originated in 1933, a particularly bad year for American education.

Every school system has copies of the *Evaluative Criteria* on file and usually schools also have them on file.

The nation is divided into six districts: Middle States, New England, North Central, Northwest, Southern and Western. Each district has a general committee. The advisory committee consists of a representative from the National Association of Secondary School Principals and the National Association of Elementary School Principals. These two ultra-liberal organizations are connected with public education, the State Department's Office of Overseas Schools and the United States Office of Education, neither of which can inspire much confidence among the patriotic elements of our nation.

It is enlightening to see some quotes from the guiding principles for the various areas of study. The following are from the *Evaluative Criteria* for Middle States high schools:

Social Studies — "The primary function is to prepare thoughtful, active citizens... in a *multicultural, rapidly changing,* and increasingly *interdependent* world... *humanistic values* should be realized through an open examination of *controversial issues* and *diverse lifestyles* ... students can inquire into questions dealing with *social values* and *behavior.*" p. 221

Home Economics — "*Modification* in the roles of men and women in both the home and employment make education for home and family life desirable for both male and female students." p. 137

English — "Literary and media works... *will promote humanistic attitudes.*" p. 101

Foreign Language — "... should foster insight into inherent *humanistic values* in an *evolving* world... assists students in adapting to the *multiethnic* environments and *value* orientations." p. 117

Health Education — "... provide learning opportunities for youth and *adults* to develop... attitudes... through courses that center on *behaviors...*" *p. 129*

Religion — "... *should include the study of God and the Person...*" p. 197

Humanism exists in the public schools throughout the nation because it is required in order for the schools to receive accreditation. Parents who want their children to grow up believing in God, loyal to their country and with a healthy attitude toward marriage and the family should *first* remove their children from the state schools and *second* go into the public schools and clean them up or close them down. Our children do not survive the pressures put on them by state education!

Train up a child in the way he should go, and when he is old he will not depart from it.
Proverbs 22:6

Parent Advocate

Behavorial psychologists, not educators, have dictated public policy and curriculum for a long time. Now they are managing our society and the American family.

At the 1982 Pro Family Forum in Dallas, Laura Rogers spoke on a new program presently in force in Missouri, home state of former President Truman who gave away our nation's top military secrets to the communists. The program is labeled Parent Advocate. The label is a perfect example of deception because the parent is the advocate's victim and the advocate is a social worker.

We learned that the behaviorists are now experimenting with how to identify a mother who is a *potential* child abuser. They observe the mother during the delivery of her baby. If the observing social worker decides the victim, i.e., the mother, is a *potential* (not a proven) child abuser, then the child is taken by the state immediately at birth. The child is withheld from the mother until she has submitted to Parent Effectiveness Training (PET). When the mother can demonstrate that she has been sufficiently "modified" then the baby will be restored to her. Submitting to brainwashing is the price the mother must pay. The mother can now be trusted to raise the child as another global/humanist clone.

My wife and I were incredulous when we heard this presentation.

The next speaker was Bill Wilson, Laura Rogers' attorney who had worked with her in trying to get the state legislature to eliminate such monstrous practices. Fortunately we got a tape of these two presentations. When the shadow of disbelief threatens to creep back, the tapes provide an irrefutable reminder that we really did hear this story about an American nightmare.

This program will eventually exist in your area. It's already in Maryland.

CHAPTER 3

Global Education
and Foundation Funding

For as he thinks within himself, so he is.
Proverbs 23:7

Education has been the major vehicle for changing the mind set of America to accept a global initiative. The process has been gradual but orchestrated. Examine any school material that concerns itself with foreign affairs or international subject matter and you will find the new global terminology of *inter-dependence* has replaced the more familiar term international which has itself replaced foreign policy.

On August 1, 1951, the 82nd Congress approved a committee to direct a thorough investigation of foundations. This committee was referred to as the Cox Committee. In its final report of January 1, 1955, the Cox Committee reported that a Moscow-directed, communist plot existed to infiltrate American foundations and to use their funds for communist purposes. (See No. 2514,

82nd Congress, 2nd session).

Congressman Reece, who served on the Cox Committee, believed that the committee was unable to complete its task and persuaded the 83rd Congress to set up another committee (the Reece Committee) to continue the investigations. Rene' A. Wormser served as counsel to the Reece Committee and authored an invaluable and interesting book, *Foundations: Their Power and Influence, The Devin-Adair Co., N.Y. 1958.*

Foundations are an interesting phenomena that allow families of immense wealth to avoid estate and other taxes while enjoying the pleasures, power and control that money can buy. It is interesting that while the Internal Revenue Service is hounding churches and bonafide Christian charities, it makes no move against these giants created for selfish motives.

Foundations are allowed to exist because the general public in effect agrees to pay more taxes on its earnings in order to allow foundation billions to go untaxed. What is the public to get in return? Charitable benefits. Foundations, therefore, should exercise the highest degree of fiduciary responsibility — but do they?

The Carnegie Endowment for International Peace Scenario

Norman Dodd was Director of Research for the Reece Committee's investigation into tax-exempt foundations of which the Carnegie Endowment is one. Parts of a speech given by Dodd in Washington, D.C., October 14, 1976, are reproduced in *The Freemen Digest* of May 1978, pp.9-11.

As part of his investigation, Dodd had received access to the minute books of the Carnegie Endowment. Those books revealed that from 1908 until 1909 the trustees of the corporation debated what would be the most effective way of changing the lifestyle of the entire nation.

Their conclusion was that war would be the most effective.

Their next question was how to involve the United States in a war so their process of change could begin. Their answer was, "We must control the diplomatic machinery of the United States."

Their next question was how to accomplish this. Their answer was, "We must control the State Department." That was 1909.

With the entrance of the United States into World War I the trustees sent a telegram to President Wilson urging him not to end the war too quickly. They could see the alteration to our national life being magnified by our participation in the conflict.

When the war was over the trustees confronted a new problem: how to prevent life in the United States from reverting back to what it was prior to 1914. Their conclusion was that they "must control education in the United States."

According to the Carnegie minute books as quoted by Dodd, the trustees divided the task between themselves and the Rockefeller Foundation. The Rockefeller Foundation would alter education pertaining to domestic subjects and the Carnegie Endowment would alter education bearing on international relations.

Together they decided that the teaching of American history must be revised. To do this, young aspirants were taken to London at the expense of the Guggenheim Foundation, which specialized in awarding fellowships, and there they were groomed in what was expected of them. When they returned they became the new force in the American Historical Society.

"This coincides with the appearance (which perhaps you will remember) of book after book, the contents of which cast aspersion on the Founders of this country, cast aspersion on the ideas which prompted the

founding of this country and relegates them to the realm of myth."
— Norman Dodd, October 14, 1976 Speech, Washington, D.C. See *The Freemen Digest,* May 1978, p. 11.

As America entered the decade of the '30s, the Commission of Social Studies of the American Historical Society issued the *Conclusions and Recommendation* (1934) report, funded by the Carnegie Corporation. Excerpts of this report can be found in Rene' A. Wormser's *Foundations,* pp. 146-148. The report states (whether true or not) that "the age of individualism and *laissez faire* in economy and governments is closing and that *a new age of collectivism* is emerging."

It goes on to say that this collectivism is one of "integration and interdependence . . . in which individual economic actions and individual property rights will be altered and abridged."

In their recommendations they call on teachers to free themselves from traditional academic pursuits and convert the schools into agencies to create a new society. The school boards were "to support a school program . . . marked by transition to some form of *socialized economy.*" *(Wormser, pp. 148,149)*

Professor Harold J. Laski, philosopher of British socialism, in his testimony to the Reece Committee, said of the Commission's report:

> *AT BOTTOM, AND STRIPPED OF ITS CAREFULLY NEUTRAL PHRASES, THE REPORT IS AN EDUCATIONAL PROGRAM FOR A SOCIALIST AMERICA.*
> — *Reece Committee Report, p. 141.*
> See *Wormser, p. 149.*

The Outlook, a social science journal for teachers, was taken over to awaken and consolidate educational leadership around the philosophy and purpose expounded in

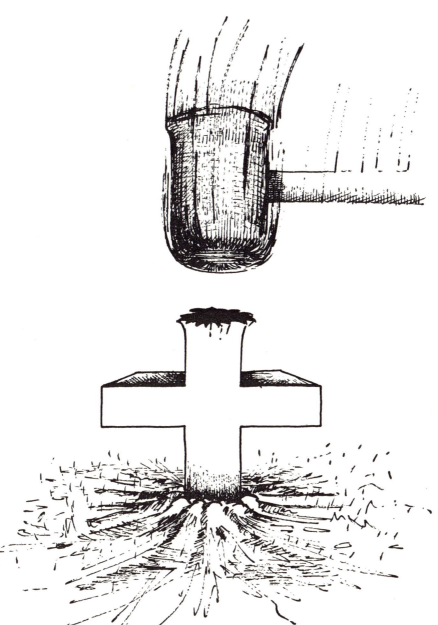

Christianity must go — one aspect of the globalists' plan.

the Commission's report. Aaron Sargent, a witness before the Reece Committee and a lawyer with considerable experience in special investigations and research in education and subversion, commented that "writers of textbooks (were) expected to revamp and rewrite their old works in accordance with this frame of reference," i.e., the Commission's report. Sargent also pointed out that "this report became the basis for a definite slanting in the curriculum by selecting certain historical facts and by no longer presenting others." (Wormser, pp. 149,150).

Are Christian Schools Safe?

Much has happened to education in America and throughout the world since this early declaration to make schools the vehicle for socialist change in American society. It should be kept in mind that education is not only secular but also religious. The seminaries and denominationally affiliated schools and colleges were also targets for the one worlders.

The Walsh Committee, created by a congressional act of August 23, 1912, to review industrial relations, also examined foundations. A number of witnesses testified that colleges had surrendered their religious identifications in order to comply with foundation requirements to receive grants, an early move by the one worlders to eliminate God from America's national life.

Two very lengthy articles in *Redbook* magazine, "The Startling Beliefs of Our Future Ministers," August 1961 and "Uproar over the Modern Ministers Beliefs," November 1961, exposed how successful the Fabian socialists (globalists today) had been in destroying Christian beliefs among seminarians. These men later filled the pulpits of America and preached heresy to their congregations. Instead of Christianity the people were taught the moral relativism of the humanists who believe that all mankind must come under a perfect one-world government created by imperfect man.

Noel Wesley Hollyfield, Jr., a graduate of the Southern Baptist Theological Seminary in Louisville, Kentucky, did an exhaustive, scholarly sociological analysis of the degrees of Christian orthodoxy among students in the seminary. This was a thesis for the master of theology degree. It was read and approved by the review committee: G. Willis Bennett, chairman, E. Glenn Hinson and Henlee Barnette, August 26, 1976, which attested to the accuracy and validity of the information and conclusions.

The following data are from Table 13.

	Diploma	M. Div.	Graduate
Belief in God.................	100.0%	71.0%	63.0%
Divinity of Jesus..............	100.0%	79.0%	63.0%
Belief in Biblical Miracles	96.0%	54.0%	37.0%
Belief in Life Beyond Death ...	100.0%	82.0%	53.0%
Belief in *Virgin Birth*	96.0%	55.0%	32.0%
Belief in the Existence of the Devil........................	96.0%	58.0%	37.0%
Belief that Jesus Walked on Water.......................	96.0%	54.0%	22.0%
Overall Averages	97.7%	64.7%	43.9%

The conclusion was that the more education the students received at Southern Seminary the less they believed in Christian orthodox beliefs. Hollyfield did a statistical comparison with a similar analysis done by Thompson at Southwestern Seminary and the Glock and Stack study of the California ministers and San Francisco laymen. Again it was confirmed that the less formal religious instruction received, the more orthodox was the Christian belief.

Globalist beliefs infiltrate the Christian schools the same way as the public schools. Most teachers and administrators in Christian schools received their training in secular, humanist colleges. Intentional or not, these attitudes, ideas, methods and techniques are all part of the package when these staff members are employed as teaching personnel.

Since the globalist program had such early beginnings, everyone living today has been humanized to some degree. It is a regrettable necessity but Christian faculties actually need to be de-programmed. The best way to do this is grounding oneself in the Word of God and know the truth. Then the error of globalism is more easily discerned when encountered. In this way we can rid ourselves of the taint of humanism and its deceptions.

Textbooks are the major vehicle for spreading globalism. Publishers will print anything they can sell, so Christian schools should be on guard when buying textbooks and other instructional materials.

Remember, too, if the Christian or private school is state accredited and the staff state certified, you are in a situation not too different from the public school. The same procedures and content are required to receive state approval.

This is why church schools must refuse state licensing and why the state boards will attack them. Conflict is inevitable. Quality of education is not the issue. Control is the issue.

State Education: Public Enemy No. 1

The American public has been deceived by the educrats. The chief aim of public education is to preserve the culture in which that educational system exists. Our schools do not do this. Education has been pre-empted to program the American people away from the fundamental principles and beliefs of our country.

The social studies curricula are the main avenues for achieving this modification in American thought and behavior. If the American people believe that this excessively expensive and inept process called education exists to secure to us and our posterity, i.e., the present and future generations of this country, our American way of life, they are mistaken.

The public schools are teaching our children to be non-Americans by fostering beliefs in global citizenship and interdependence. Public schools do not promote a healthy, national loyalty to traditional American ideals. They do not encourage an allegiance to the United States. Few school children even say the pledge to the flag and many don't bother to stand for the national anthem. Our children's values have been successfully modified. Public education doesn't inspire our children to love and respect the hard-won heritage of freedom, individualism and self-determination — The American Dream. Few school children have ever heard of The American Dream.

But our values have been modified, too. The very things against which our forefathers fought, such as freedom from burdensome taxation and religious oppression, we accept as the norm in our lives today.

According to Michael Loyd Chadwick, editor of *The Freemen Digest,* the major agency in orchestrating this subversion of American loyalty has been the National Education Association (NEA), largest and one of the most powerful lobbies in the United States. Although the subverting of American allegiance was begun before World War I by an elite of powerful Americans with international interests, it did not become an overt policy of the NEA until after World War II.

In 1948 the NEA issued a volume entitled *Education for International Understanding in American Schools.* The militancy of the NEA's indoctrination of school children with one-world beliefs occasioned the Reece Committee mentioned earlier to investigate the NEA and to admonish the Association about fostering global concepts among American school children. (Wormser, p. 216)

In 1975 the NEA published a bicentennial program in

Today's Education, the official NEA publication, entitled "A Declaration of Interdependence: Education for a Global Community." The very first proposal in the declaration called for the development of a global curriculum.

In 1976 the NEA endorsed and published in *Today's Education,* (March-April, 1976, pp. 86,87) "A Declaration of Interdependence" commissioned by the World Affairs Council of Philadelphia and written by Dr. Henry Steele Commager, revisionist historian, teacher and staff member of the Aspen Institute for Humanistic Studies in Colorado. This document was signed in Independence Hall in Philadelphia by some 125 congressmen in violation of their oath of office. (See *Freemen* Digest, May 1978, p. 45).

In June of 1976 NEA former presidents Helen D. Wise and James A. Harris made the following comment concerning educators and their potential role in the developing new world order or global community:

> "It is with . . . sobering awareness that we set about to CHANGE the course of American education for the twenty-first century by embracing the ideals of global community, the equality and interdependence of all peoples and nations, and education as a tool . . ." (See *NEA,* The Freemen Digest, September, 1978, p. 2).

The Office of International Relations — which works closely with the State Department, a variety of international organizations, the United Nations and especially UNESCO — has translated these sentiments into NEA policies. (The United States just withdrew from UNESCO because of its anti-American stance since its creation).

On January 27-30, 1982, in New York City a conference was held to teach teachers in the field of social studies what to teach. (A similar conference was held in Baltimore in 1983). This Mid-Atlantic Regional Conference for the Social Studies had a hundred workshops: thirty-three specifically dealt with teaching globalism, eighteen were concerned with secondary topics supportive of globalism and twenty-five espoused values questionable to traditional American principles. Some of the workshop titles were:

> Global Education — A Population Perspective
> The Family Structure in a Global Setting
> The Basics of Global Responsibility
> How to Run A World
> Global History
> Citizenship for a Global Age
> Global Education
> Evolutionary Education, etc.

In the January 1982 issue of *Social Education*, the monthly publication of the NEA's National Council of Social Studies, the following position statement was made on global education:

> "Human life has been globalized ... The view of the world as a collection of countries pursuing separate destinies is no longer accurate ... The purpose of global education is to develop in youth the knowledge, skills, and *attitudes* needed ... in a world possessing limited natural resources ... and increasing interdependence ... (S)ocial Studies teachers are in a key position to play a leading role in bringing a global perspective to the school curriculum ..."
> (pp. 36, 37)

We are still being deceived!

Do not move the ancient boundary which your fathers have set.
                    Proverbs 22:28

CHAPTER 4

More About Public Enemy No. 1 Public Education

The fear of the Lord is the beginning of knowledge:
Fools despise wisdom and instruction.
Proverbs 1:7

The National Level

The World Affairs Council was created in 1949 with its main office on the third floor gallery of the John Wanamaker Store in Philadelphia. It was created by merging the Philadelphia branch of the Foreign Policy Association with the United Nations Council. The United Nations Council initially was set up to sell the United Nations to the American people and keep us in that organization, thereby avoiding a repeat of the League of Nations scenario.

The purpose of the World Affairs Council is global education. The Council is well organized and has been indoctrinating pupils, teachers and the public in the acceptance of the "new world order." It developed such a multitude of educational programs that it created an outreach, the National Council of Community Affairs Organizations, in each of the states just to monitor the programs.

The programs are geared to four levels: elementary, junior high, senior high and special education. The Council fosters high school international relations clubs, provides classroom and club speakers on international topics and gives individuals free subscriptions to *Newsweek, Time* and *The New York Times.* Special trips to the United Nations are planned with briefs by Council members who emphasize the interdependence of nations.

In the spring high school participants get to act out a Council activity called Model United Nations Program. The pupils begin preparing for this in January and spend three days role playing as global architects.

In 1976, in cooperation with the Philadelphia School District, the Council developed the *Interdependence Curriculum Aid.* You can get a copy of this by writing to World Affairs Council, Third Floor Gallery, John Wanamaker Store, 13th and Market Streets, Philadelphia, PA 19107 and sending $3. Be sure to examine the section entitled "World Law and International Institutions." In this section are the suggestions:

> That a world constitutional convention draft a world constitution as occurred in 1787 for the United States,
> That national sovereignty must be limited . . . if the human species is to survive,
> That all nations must give up defense armaments and submit to a world police force and a world court, and
> That a world revenue service be created to collect taxes from all nations."

On the international or global level the World Affairs

Council is a very prestigious organization. The *Creme de la creme* of the global society turn out in black tie when the Council presents the international Statesman's Award at its State Dinner.

The first award was presented to the founder of the Bilderbergers, His Royal Highness Prince Bernard of the Netherlands, amid a glittering gala of trumpets and tulips. The "outstanding" qualities and influence of Kurt Waldheim, United Nations Secretary General, also have been recognized by the Council as well as Henry Kissinger, himself a Bilderberger and staff member of the Aspen Institute for Humanistic Studies. The State Dinner is only one of many international socials conducted by the Council.

The wicked strut about on every side, When vileness is exalted among the sons of men.
                    Psalm 12:8

For higher education, i.e., college level, the University of Pennsylvania, in collaboration with the World Affairs Council, organized the Global Interdependence Center. Its mission is to indoctrinate students, professors and the American public in the new world order. A current emphasis which is especially dangerous for the United States is the movement to subject our nation to the dictates of the Third World powers.

The objective of such propaganda is to program the United States to accept a re-distribution of our national wealth to ungodly nations. In the last fifteen years the Third World or Group of 77 (which now exceeds 100 nations) has gained tremendous power in the United Nations. These nations have created a whole new set of international institutions to deal with *economic equity,* in particular the New International Economic Order.

Check section fifteen of the *Humanist Manifesto II* in the appendix, "... extreme disproportions in wealth, in-

The Tangled Web of Deception.

come, and economic growth should be REDUCED on a worldwide basis."

The State Level

On the state level the school situation is just as much out of hand as on the national level. The general public still has a lot of power on the local level but usually is unaware of what is going on because they are still in the crisis management ploy which locks a sizeable segment of our work force into unemployment and public assistance lines.

Such people aren't going to be interested in talks about public-versus-church education and the virtues of George Washington. They will accept almost anything that promises them a solution to their problems just like during the Great Depression.

Socialist programs which would have been anathema to the American people in 1928 were embraced wholeheartedly in the 1930s. Unemployment, recessions and depressions are not accidents. They are planned and their intent is to manipulate large segments of the population just as the phony energy crisis did. (See chapter 7). These programmed crises work very well. The unemployment crisis got a lot of adults back into school for skills retraining as well as another dose of values clarification and behavior modification.

The Shell Game: Beware of Bylaw Mandate Power

Is a man standing in an unemployment line in Maryland going to listen to a discourse on why the Federal Reserve should be abolished? He is going to be less interested in a harangue about the Maryland State School Board wanting to make a policy change. Like the people in other states he trusts the educrats to do their job and educate his children while he tries to keep food on the table, clothes on his family and a roof over their heads — even if he has to get rid of both cars. It is easy to manipulate the public when they are pre-occupied with "basic" concerns.

Previously if an educational measure was to be binding on all the local subdivisions in Maryland, it had to be introduced into the state legislature and approved by the state assembly. This gave the public an opportunity for public hearings and participation. Convinced by the Maryland State School Board that they are the experts in such matters and not the legislators, the Board, despite the fact that they created an expensive school system that taught the children how NOT to read and write, got the legislature to give the Board bylaws the same force as an act of legislation. In effect this nullified the power of every local school board and placed all decision-making power in the hands of the State Board. As a consequence we now have MSDE Goal No. 4.

Goal No. 4 of the Maryland State Department of Education requries every child in the Maryland public school system be taught to believe in interdependence and globalism — whether the parents want it or not — beginning in the kindergarten through the twelfth grades (K-12). If your State Board of Education doesn't already have bylaw mandate, it soon will.

Another State Board mandate was Project Basic. Every state has a Project Basic program, but it may be called by another name. Most of the local boards in Maryland object to the program because it is costly, time consuming and of no academic benefit, but there is nothing they can do about it except pay the bill. The overt rationale is that education is going back to "the basics" so kids can learn to read and write but it is business as usual — operant conditioning or affective education. The program was designed by Benjamin Bloom, the same educrat who wrote the Elementary and Secondary Education Act (ESEA) that taught the kids how NOT to read and write by keeping them occupied with games and "fun."

If education and entertainment were meant to be the same, they wouldn't be spelled differently.

The covert objective behind Project Basic is to establish a policing and monitoring system. The model was instituted in 1971 by the NEA and commonly referred to as PPBES, or planning, programming, budgeting and evaluation system. It is also called Management by Objective or MBO. It is a method of delineating all performance and programming to computer processing. In this way every child and teacher will be tracked by computer to monitor who is teaching the globalist program and who is or is not being successfully indoctrinated.

The Computer Connection

Computers will allow every local school system to be patched into a state curriculum which will interface with a national and eventually a global network. The opening line of the NEA Bicentennial Ideabook Program 1 reads: "Volume 1 will contain a reframing of the cardinal principles of education and recommendation for a *global curriculum*," (See *NEA*, Freemen Digest, September 1978, p.66). It isn't a coincidence that the state and federal educrats in the 1970s decided to create the National Diffusion Network (NDN) with $9 million of Title III, ESEA funds. The purpose of the NDN is to create a national curriculum. Private and church schools will be included.

After the Bob Jones University decision and the Nebraska Seven national disgrace, it looks like the courts will require religious schools to submit, regardless of doctrinal beliefs. The intent is that all schools will be nationalized and removed from local control.

The programs disseminated by the NDN are also business as usual: affective education, i.e., values clarification, behavior modification, humanistic attitudes, life-transforming change agentry, etc.

One of their programs is *New Model Me*, a program known to all veteran fighters against affective education. How does the NDN decide which programs to disseminate? They use the "mastery learning" techniques of Benjamin Bloom of Project Basic and ESEA fame. (See *The National Educator*, March 1982, P.13). Each state has an NDN "facilitator" who makes these programs known to the local educational agencies (LEA).

Project BEST is another curious program funded by your tax dollars ($855,282) through a federal grant (#300-81-0421). Project Best stands for Basic Education Skills Through Technology and was written by the Association for Educational Communication and Technology (AECT), an NEA spin-off. The purpose of the project is to teach LEAs how to write their own grants so they can purchase computers and software with federal funds.

Throughout the grant and particularly on pages 1.5 and 2.2 are references to "intangible benefits and changes in behavior or attitude that result from participation in the project" and "Other perceived changes in the behavior of youth."

Although the elaborations on "improving" behavior sound good, the method is *consensus*, that is, the right or wrong of behavior can be variable according to majority standards or public policy.

It was the *consensus* opinion that lost the Bob Jones University case. In other words, moral relativism or situation ethics would prevail, and behavior would improve statistically if the *consensus*, which is always programmed, decided that a particular "bad" behavior was no longer bad. For example, decriminalizing the use of marijuana, which the NEA supports, would statistically create the impression that drug abuse was on the decline.

Chistians beware: if monitoring text books was tough, just try monitoring national computerized curricula!

Problem: since basic education has not been taught for years, it is now a national concern.

Solution: Project Best will make it possible for state and local education agencies to tap into a national information bank such as the affective, mind-bending Project Basic or PLATO.

Change: *national* secularized curriculum would be in place. To insure teacher participation a requirement for continuing certification could — and will — require teacher accreditation in educational technology and micro-computers.

An interesting aside is that every member of the Project Best Advisory Board is either associated with the Ford Foundation, has international educational connections, a lifetime membership in NEA and/or has a background in social engineering or behavioral psychology. Do you get the impression that our cards are coming from a stacked deck?

What About ED?

We have no friends in the Department of Education in Washington. Department Secretary Terrell Bell is an avid admirer of computers and educational technology. In fact he has publicly stated that by the year 2000 text-books will be obsolete.

Although President Ronald Reagan chose Bell to dis-mantle the Department of Education (ED), which was created by President Carter as a reward to the NEA for their support in the 1976 election, the department has only become bigger. Bell's proposal to replace the de-partment with a Foundation for Educational Assistance could be worse considering past experience with founda-tions. Bell has already begun hiding the NDN (See *The National Educator,* March, 1982, p. 13) within the Ten Federal Regions that were created unconstitutionally during the Nixon administration — and continued by

President Carter — to replace the fifty states.

The Seven Cardinal _____ (fill in the blank)

In 1918 the NEA published a report of the Commission on the Reorganization of Secondary Education in which "the seven cardinal principles made their first appearance." (See *Today's Education,* September-October, 1976, an interesting parallel to the seven cardinal sins). Nine years later the National Congress of Parents and Teachers incorporated them into its permanent platform and affirmed that these principles had become "the objectives not only of the high school, but of all education."

In September 1975 a Bicentennial Preplanning Committee retained the seven goals even after sixty years. In brief they were (1) health, (2) command of fundamental processes, (3) worthy home membership, (4) vocation, (5) citizenship, (6) worthy use of leisure and (7) ethical character. Regrettably these goals are a smoke screen to cover humanistic and globalistic goals and objectives.

The makeup of the Preplanning Committee and the Cardinal Principles Panel should be of some interest to us. The co-chairs were the former NEA Presidents James A. Harris and Helen D. Wise, whom we have quoted earlier as calling for the teaching of a new world order, global community and interdependence. Another name of special interest is that of Terrell H. Bell who at that time was just a U.S. Office of Education employee.

On the Panel was:

★ futurist Roy C. Amara, president, Institute for the Future, program committeeman for World Future Society Assembly;

★ futurist Benjamin Bloom, designer of ESEA legislation, and Project Basic, and promoter of the operant conditioning technique of mastery learning, which is the core of Project Basic;

★ McGeorge Bundy of the Ford Foundation. The Ford

Foundation has a long history of supporting globalism. (See testimony of former Assistant Secretary of State Spruille Braden to Rene' Wormser, *Foundations,* p. 212).

★ Norman Cousins, *Saturday Review,* humanist, population control advocate and honorary chairman of Planetary Citizens, member of People for the American Way (Norman Lear's group), ACLU, World Futurist USA, Council on Foreign Relations (CFR) and adjunct professor of the Medical Humanities, University of California School of Medicine, Los Angeles;

★ Willis W. Harman, co-director of the Stanford Research Institute (SRI), now senior social scientist, Strategic Environment Center, SRI International, professor of Engineering Economics Systems at Stanford University, board of directors of Planetary Citizens and author of future studies, program committeeman for World Future Society Assembly, president of the Institute of Noetic Studies and speaker at the 1982 annual meeting of the Association for Humanistic Psychology on "Values and Spirit in Global Disarmament";

★ Rev. Theodore M. Hesburg, president of Notre Dame University, Planetary Citizens, member of the National Advisory Council of ACLU, Pope John Paul II's Pontifical Council for Culture, advisory board of National Peace Academy Campaign, staff member of the Aspen Institute for Humanistic Studies, trustee of Chase Manhattan Bank. (Rockefeller bank), chairman Rockefeller Foundation, Council on Foreign Relations (CFR), etc;

★ Norman Lear, Board of Advocates for Planned Parenthood Federation of America, Inc., "Secular Pope of Entertainment T.V." (*Human Events,* August 1, 1981), founder of People for the American Way (PAW), the board of which is a study in itself of the enemies of Christian morality and American principles;

★ David Rockefeller, Chase Manhattan Bank, Chairman of CFR and Trilateral Commission and Bilderberger member.

You can find the same globalist bias in the credentials of a majority of major education panels or study groups.

Some comments from the Committee and Panel were:

★ "I see the seven cardinal principles becoming skills for *survival.*"

– Donald Blakeslee, Wyoming teacher

★ "... there should be increased emphasis on *life-long learning.*"

– Helen D. Wise, Pennsylvania teacher, former NEA president

★ "We should think in terms of forward to the basics rather than back to the basics. *The new basics* will include the attainment of *decision-making skills in human relationships.*" (Same old affective values education).

– Grace C. Baisinger, National Congress of Parents and Teachers.

★ "Some of our old concepts of success have actually become a threat to our survival in an increasingly *crowded world.*" (Globalist Malthusian theory).

– Lester R. Brown, Worldwatch Institute

★ "I would prefer to change the 'worthy use of leisure time' to the 'creative use of *leisure time.*'" (Even use of leisure time will be programmed in the Fabian or globalist society).

– Sally Swing, United Nations

★ "I see missing from the cardinal principles references to the *aesthetic experience* ..." ("Cultural" courses are presently being considered for a mandate).

– Sterling McMurrin, University of Utah

★ "The seven cardinal principles are fine — but only if WE *interpret* them in the context of the *future* rather than in their *past* setting." (No Comment!)

– David Rockefeller, Chase Manhattan Bank

★ "I hope that by 2000 A.D. education is going to a *multiethnic process* from which each of us profits

from the best of the *other cultures.*" (Comparative Cultures — are one world).
– Lloyd Elm, Institute for the Development of Law

It isn't difficult to see how education today is a fulfilling of these principles: survival skills are a required subject; community education and the president's report on schools are pushing for cradle-to-grave or life-long education; basics today are "new" basics and not the basics we want; survival in a "crowded world" is an on-going indoctrination; leisure education is pending as a mandate as well as aesthetic experience; all instruction is open for interpretation and separation from the past; and the anarchy of multiethnic and cultural studies is subtly destroying American patriotism. We know too well just how much emphasis has been given to the seven principles.

Teachers should wake up to the fact that the present abortion rate plus computer education will eliminate them as a profession, reducing them to mere "facilitators" of which only a few will be needed.

Trust in the Lord with all your heart, And do not lean on your own understanding. In all your ways acknowledge Him, And He will make your paths straight.
Proverbs 3:5,6

CHAPTER 5

Think Globally, Act Locally:
Caveat Emptor

This or a similar scenario is being duplicated in every state and probably in most western nations.

In a letter dated December 2, 1981, to School Board President David Daneker, Council President Walter Orlinsky of the Baltimore City Council wrote, "The City of Baltimore is a large old industrial city in a nation which is squarely in the midst of the *post industrial society*... We can make Baltimore as important to this new emerging America as it was to the industrial giant of the past. This can be accomplished in one way and in one way alone. That way is to *produce a generation* of young people at home in the ways of *post-industrial society*... This means a generation of children who are comfortable with high technology, computers, and all that they imply (Does he mean Big Brother?)... this you seem to be doing with your new *five-year plan.*"

The globalists consider the present period in America's history to be the post-industrial society. This is true because the globalists are powerful policy makers. They have made the United States a post-industrial nation because they need an information society with which to regulate the new world order.

Have all of our resources suddenly disappeared? Has our working force suddenly forgotten all their skills and talents? Have Americans suddenly stopped needing manufactured items? If none of these things has happened why are we in an economic slump?

The Federal Reserve was created to prevent such economic dislocations from happening — but they still happen. This means one of two things: either the Federal Reserve doesn't work and can't prevent these disasters from happening or the Federal Reserve causes these things to happen. Either of these eventualities justify getting rid of the Federal Reserve.

Dr. Debra Freeman, a director of the National Anti-Drug Coalition (Mid-Atlantic Region) is a bitter opponent of the Five Year Plan and insists it is part of the globalist conspiracy. She points out that David Daneker, the Baltimore School Board president, was former Senator Joseph Tydings' aide when Senator Tydings fostered a series of conferences on education reform which brought in values education, survival skills and functionalism. Today Tydings is best known for his international campaign as a leader of the Population Crisis Committee to reduce the world's population through implementation of Global 2000.

The latest mandate under consideration is "required voluntary" (?) community service of one hundred hours before seniors can graduate. The contradiction of terms never bothers enlightened educrats but this mandate violates section 1 of Article 13 to the Constitution: "Neither slavery nor involuntary servitude, except as a punishment for crime . . . shall exist within the United States . . ."

The overt rationale sounds good, "raise the consciousness level of public education graduates to community service," but this is the same requirement in the Russian and Communist Chinese educational systems. If you want to know the future "trends" being programmed for American education, examine the Communist Chinese system. It's the global model being copied by the American educrats.

The covert rationale behind this mandate seems fairly obvious. It will put the state in control of the graduating pupils so they can be socialized or community-ized through "community service," free labor for the state or for institutions with semi-governmental services. No matter how flexible and diverse the community service may be, it gives unconstitutional control over the lives of our children. It intrudes into an area of no genuine educational merit and it promotes the community school objective which has never been explained to the American public. So obviously the American public has had no say in its development and will have no part in the decision to implement it.

In his testimony to justify the community service mandate to the State Board of Education, State Superintendent Hornbeck quoted from Carnegie-funded Ernie Boyer's book *High School* that "to be fully human one must serve." (Hornbeck Memorandum to MSDE, January 25, 1984).

Does this mean if you don't do what the State tells you to do you aren't fully human? If the terminology sounds somewhat familiar, it was the same argument used by the abortionists to justify eliminating the unborn and by Hitler to get rid of the "useless eater" who could not contribute to the Third Reich. God considers us "fully human" at conception.

Thine eyes have seen my unformed substance; And in Thy book they were all written, The days that were ordained

for me, When as yet there was not one of them.
Psalm 139:16

Your state may already have the mandated community service, but if not, it will.

What's A Community School?

At last the public schools will be put back into the neighborhood setting so the parents can be assured that education will concern itself with academic and vocational instruction, right? Wrong!

Begin scrutinizing whether community school programs are being discussed in your area, because "sooner or later they're gonna' be coming around." Keep in mind a few of the rules of thumb already discussed.
1) conflict, resolution, change or create a problem, advertise the problem, provide your solution to the problem
2) covert and overt rationales –
3) finally, global speak, i.e., they aren't saying what you think they are saying. For example, when the educrats speak of "community life," they don't mean what goes on in the neighborhood. They mean communal living.

When I first heard about community education and community schools I was attending a Maryland Association of Counties (MACO) meeting in December of 1983 at Hunt Valley, Md. The speaker was a representative from the Office of the State Superintendent of Education. My interest was piqued by the fact that the speaker's sponsor was the Bureau of Parks and Recreation, not the Department of Education.

The programs involved were geared so much to replacing the parents instead of providing recreational activities that my conscience finally forced me to raise some questions about this intrusion upon parental rights.

At one point the speaker answered by saying that the

state school superintendent believes he owns fifty percent of every child in the state. When I loudly demanded to know when the parents of Maryland had agreed to this ridiculous presumption, the moderator, who had merely been an emcee until the questions began, quickly brought the presentation to a close.

One of the county representatives present said there would be no parks and recreation program for his county if community education didn't make the school facilities available to his department. He had to agree with me that without the county's taxes there would be no schools so why shouldn't Parks and Rec. have access to such public facilities. He did express one significant concern about the financial arrangements of the program.

When the program began all the money went to Parks and Recreation for recreational activities. The second year 25 percent went to the community education program, 50 percent the next year and presently the recreation department is fighting to get any of the money because the state superintendent wants it all for the sensitivity classes and PET type programs.

Now that the public schools have taught every child he is a law unto himself and there is no right or wrong, our crime rate has skyrocketed in order to feed the drug and other habits debilitating our youth. To counter this upsurge of criminality we need neighborhood watches to safeguard our lives and property — at least that's an overt rationale. Another way (covert?) to look at the neighborhood watch is it gets us to spy on one another, we inventory our valuables for the authorities and we have block captains and neighborhood councils — just like in Communist Cuba. Well, since the law won't let us protect ourselves, and the law can't protect us, we need something; so we accept the neighborhood watch, set up with the best of intentions by our neighbors and local police. What has this to do with community schools?

When Community Education (the philosophy) and the Community School (the physical facility) are fully in place, the schools will be the core of all community activity. The children will live at the school. In one of the Washington, D.C. suburban counties the dormitories are already under construction. Block captains will be appointed to make sure all children are attending the community school. If your children do not attend, you will be reported to the block council (Interdepartmental Community Education Council) before which you must appear and prove yourself innocent of child neglect for not having your child in the community school. Note that like other cases of child abuse and neglect the parent is presumed GUILTY and must prove innocence. Quite a turn around from the American principle that all men shall be presumed innocent until *proven* guilty. Again, beware of undefined or open-ended child abuse or child neglect laws.

By the time community education is in place there are to be no home schools, church schools or private schools, so it will be rare for a child to be in a non-community school. Also, the parents themselves will be fully involved with the community school.

"The major goals of Community Education are: greater inter-agency cooperation in the planning and delivery of services; maximum utilization of physical, financial and *human resources,* particularly school buildings; improved and expanded *programming for all ages;* and citizens participation in the local decision-making and problem-solving processes." — *Community Education Proven Practices,* Department of Education, State of New Jersey, 1979, p.2.

"Buyer beware" seems an appropriate label for this educational trap. Despite all the good-sounding phrases there are some real dangers. The only citizen participation intended in this program is that of a victim in a concentration camp — "dissident camps" is the euphemism for the

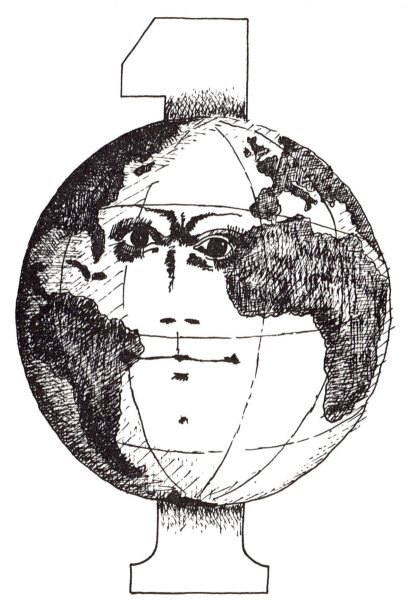

Globalism — One World

ten concentration camps our government presently maintains, one dissident camp in each of the regions. The government will do the planning and run the show. The citizen-inmates or patients will contribute by following orders.

The basic concept of community school is that education is a *lifelong* process and takes place everywhere and all the time. (Sounds OK). Services are provided to all age groups.

The first passage of Federal Community Education legislation was in 1976, the year the Declaration of Interdepence was signed. New Jersey and North Carolina evidently are front runners at present in focusing on multiple uses of school facilities. It's easy to see how Parks and Rec. would be an easy way to slip such a program in by the back door.

With everyone under the auspices of the government schools and dependent on them for recreation and leisure, training and *every* imaginable service — the facilities will be open around the clock, every day of the year — community education will place every one under the indoctrination of the New Age globalists. If the private citizen doesn't go along, he will find himself and his family without many vital services now taken for granted — or in a camp for dissidents.

What other good things do the educrats have planned for us?

The Global Awareness Council

The county council to which I was elected has six district council members and a council president. Shortly after I was elected I introduced three resolutions: one requested that school counselors involve parents in pregnancy and abortion counseling with minor females in the public schools; another requested that the School Board make public school facilities available on a rental basis to churches and church groups on the same basis as other community groups; and the third resolution created a family preservation commission to study the problems of family preservation that might be caused by government actions or policies.

The first two resolutions were passed with only one dissenting vote, that of the council president. The third resolution passed with all seven votes but trouble developed when the council president nominated the founder of the county's Planned Parenthood chapter and another council member nominated the wife of the county's ACLU head to serve on the commission.

Since neither of these nominees understood the biblical concept of the traditional American family, there was strong objection to their nominations. They were eventually voted onto the commission on the argument that no commission should include only Christians because a diversity of points of view was needed. Although many county agencies and commissions exist without a Christian perspective, the reverse was unthinkable.

At the same time that the voting and debating of the three resolutions were going on, I received a membership list for a local group sponsored by the county's community college, the Council on Global Awareness. It was a small list of limited memberships, less than thirty names, but the names were significant. It included the president of the Harford County Council (a Republican) and the head of the Harford County Republican Central Committee; Mr. and Mrs. Harford County ACLU; Mr. and Mrs. Harford County Planned Parenthood, (both of whom were pushed on the Family Preservation Commission by the County Council president); the superintendent of Harford County Schools, his deputy superintendent and the director of curriculum who has now moved on to the State Department of Education; the director of Harford County Libraries; the president of the Harford Community College and some of his staff members; the director of the State Department of Education's health services; president of the School Board; chairman of the Citizen's Advisory Board (Education); the member of the Harford County delegation to the state legislature who also fostered the latchkey centers despite parent rejection of the program; former principal of the Harford County Day Care Center; the Harford County American Association of University Women; the League of Women Voters; chairman of the County Council of PTAs; and the YMCA. For a small rural county this is quite a global network of all the educational facilities and child-centered agencies.

World Control: Its Past Performance

The globalists, indifferent to the destruction they have caused to Christian principles, the American family and our great nation, believe they know and are doing what is best for the people of the world. Everything is secondary to achieving their end goal of one world or global control.

Looking at the past performance of the people leading these programs at all levels — national, state and local — should make everyone shudder, including the proponents of globalism, when they realize that their fate and that of future generations will be in the hands of such morally depraved, evil people. Whether it is Herod, Hitler or Humanism, the bottom line is the same: death — death of opposing individuals, death of dissident groups, death of nationalistic populations, death of the unborn, disabled, retarded and untrained.

CHAPTER 6

Zero Population and Public Education

Since Zero Population advocates, globalists, Fabians, New Agers, and others are the same, they follow the same successful formula to get what they want: conflict, resolution, change, *or* create a problem, advertise the problem, solve the problem. Every statement they make on population is premised on *overpopulation* and *population crisis*.

Run your own test about overpopulation. Look in a world almanac, an atlas or encyclopedia and find out how many half-acres of land exist in the United States. (The information is probably in full acres so just double that figure to get the half-acres). Divide into the number of half-acres the world's population, 4.5 billion. You will discover that everyone in the world could fit into the United States, each with a half-acre, and there would still be 60,000,000 full acres unused plus all the rest of the world. You can do the same thing with Jacksonville, Fla. and square footage.

In February 1982 Linus Pauling, twice winner of the Nobel Prize (Chemistry 1954 and Peace 1962), a Planetary Citizen, Humanist of the Year in 1962 and national chairman of the Population Action Council, sent a letter to public school principals "in the hope that you can help circulate the attached letter to those of your colleagues who might have an interest in global population issues..."

The program being launched was Educators Who Care, implying that educators who might disagree are uncaring. The objective was "to bring population concerns into the classroom" through high school, college and university staff members and generate a "U.S. leadership commitment to bring population into balance with resources." This is the exact intent of the globalists as stated in *Global 2000 Report to the President*, the Malthusian theory of surplus population and limited resources.

The Population Action Council is a division of the Population Institute, Suite 209, 110 Maryland Avenue N.E., Washington, D.C. 20002, (202) 544-3303. The director is Werner Fornos. The Council "is funded by grants and private and corporate contributions, but neither receives nor seeks funding from the United States Government. All contributions are tax deductible."

The Council also has a special non-profit postage permit (#41127). Tax deductible status is in itself government aid. So are special postage rates. If the grants are from foundations, which I strongly suspect they are, then these funds also come from an untaxed source, which is government assistance.

Large school systems such as Baltimore have separate departments to deal with population education but the only point of view presented is *overpopulation crisis.*

THE POPULATION ACTION COUNCIL
110 Maryland Avenue NE ● Washington DC 20002 ● (202) 544-8400   Cable: POPINST Washington D

February 1982

Rec'd 3-8-82

Linus Pauling
National Chairman
Marc Maire
Alabama
Andrea R C. Helms
Alaska
Steven K. Happle
Arizona
Howard G. Stephens
Arkansas
John D. Maguire
California
Sherry Manning
Colorado
Bruce Russett
Connecticut
Marvin D. Sussman
Delaware
Roch L. Mirabeau
Florida
John T. Ozby
Georgia
Y. Scott Matsumoto
Hawaii
James W. Tumpkins
Idaho
Brian Barry
Illinois
Lynton K. Caldwell
Indiana
Rev. C. Joseph O'Hara
Iowa
Linda Richter
Kansas
Amiya K. Mohanty
Kentucky
Kenneth L. Smith
Louisiana
Sonya O. Rose
Maine
William Alcott
Maryland
B.F. Skinner
Massachusetts
Deborah Oakley
Michigan
R.S. Schwartz
Minnesota
M. El Attar
Mississippi
Francis C. Gamelin
Missouri
John M. Mcquiston
Montana
Lynn White
Nebraska
Mrs. Frances Saxton
Nevada
James W. Hammond
New Hampshire
Ashley Montagu
New Jersey
Richard Tomasson
New Mexico
Hans A. Bethe
New York
Betty Lugowski
North Carolina
Willis H. Truesdell
North Florida
Lawrence Brown
Ohio
Gary D. Sandefur
Oklahoma
Lawrence R. Carter
Oregon
Herbert A. Simon
Pennsylvania
Basu Zimmer
Rhode Island
W. Ben Nesbit
South Carolina
Joseph Irish
South Dakota
Alma Walker
Tennessee
Luther H. Evans
Texas
Levi D. Bean
Utah
Neil S. Allen Sr.
Vermont
Layton David Henry
Virginia
Shirley B. Gordon
Washington
Roger H. Trent
West Virginia
Jean Silk
Wisconsin
Judith Davenport
Wyoming
Irving Spitzberg Jr.
District of Columbia
Ernest Boyer
District of Columbia

Barbery Byfield
National Coordinator

Dear Colleague,

Educators have an enormous responsibility in the communication of knowledge about our world and its destiny. The challenge involves presenting the hard cold facts of perhaps the most serious threat to world stability--overpopulation.

In the two short decades between now and the end of the century, world population is expected to grow from the present 4.5 billion people to more than 6 billion. Ninety percent of this growth will occur in the poorest, least developed countries of the world. Clearly this kind of growth will outpace any strides the great majority of these countries will be able to make toward improving the quality of life for their people.

Educators must continue to help people become aware of the forces that shape their lives. This awareness must be channeled into the ability to make responsible decisions about issues of global importance. The Population Action Council has resolved to bring population concerns into the classroom and to this end is undertaking a grass roots educational campaign. Educators Who Care, through its participants in high schools, colleges and universities across the country, is aiming to provide the impetus for a dynamic U.S. leadership commitment to bring population into balance with resources.

I am asking that you join our efforts in this vitally important project. If you have any questions, please feel free to get in touch with Barbery Byfield, National Coordinator, at 202-544-8400. Your involvement is needed by this generation and the ones still to come.

Sincerely,

Linus Pauling

Linus Pauling

A DIVISION OF THE POPULATION INSTITUTE

Death Education

Most parents that I have spoken to are unaware that their children have or are taking death education. Many pupils who have taken it also are unaware because they believe they were in a creative writing or similar project. If you ask the children such questions as, "Have you ever done a grave rubbing or written your epitaph or obituary?" you can expect a "yes" answer. Some will have visited mortuaries and graveyards, lain in the bottom of an open grave, observed part of an embalming procedure, even touched a dead body at a funeral home.

The overt justification is that everyone will at some point encounter the emotional impact of death due to the death of a relative, loved one, or close associate, and since the funeral home industry has been "exposed" by a number of talk shows as taking advantage of grief stricken relatives, the public via school children must be educated about this prospect.

In the eyes of the futurists the ever-neglectful home fails to prepare the child for these eventualities, so the government schools in their eagerness to control the "whole person" of the child have taken over this role. Yet, death education and thanatology came into existence in government schools without any parental or community input or knowledge.

(If the globalists have their way with zero population programs, they can guarantee everyone will experience some contact with death, one way or another. The humanistic one worlders have a low regard for human life).

The public and particularly parents of school children need to remember that in affectual teaching the child not only learns the thesis but also the antithesis, i.e., the opposite. The child doesn't just learn a single precept even though only one point of view may be taught.

Teachers are guilty of forgetting this too, and it is for this reason that many sincere teachers are unaware of their participation in globalist behavior modification. When they present "all or both" sides of an argument they unwittingly employ behavior modification. In good conscience these Christian and patriotic teachers will angrily protest against attacks on public education as being unfounded.

Consider this: a child is taught about overpopulation in a current events class and abortion in a science unit, writes his obituary in creative writing, is involved in a values clarification process in psychology, participates in a survival game, role plays as a global architect in a Model United Nations program, is forced into home economics instead of auto shop, and on and on the days, weeks, months and years roll by. The child is coming up with a complete globalist mindset, whereas the teacher who deals only with a segment of the child's schedule is unaware that a unit or lesson in his curriculum contributed to the teaching of a hidden agenda buried in the total educational program of the child.

Now that teachers and society have been programmed to accept humanistic values the new interdisciplinary and interdepartmental emphasis currently being pushed will be acceptable and will speed up the cloning of upcoming generations of humanists.

Let's look at this subject from a different point of view than that of the educrat.

Who are some of the groups behind death education? Planned Parenthood, Cremation Association of America, Euthanasia Education Council and the National Funeral Directors Association help textbook publishers put out books for this program.

U.S. Senator Zorinsky, testifying before the Senate Subcommittee on Education, said such courses as *Living With Dying* insinuated that a belief in life after death was unrealistic and had caused school children to experience nightmares and even physical distress because of the fixation caused by the death education course.

Barbara Morris, in her booklet *Religion of Humanism in Public Schools*, says death ed causes conflict for children from homes that stress traditional moral values.

In these courses the children are confronted with such questions as:

★How often do you think about your own death?

★If you could choose, when would you die?

★When you think of your own death how do you feel?

★How often have you seriously contemplated committing suicide?

★If you were to commit suicide, what method would you probably use?

★When is suicide justifiable?

Such teaching fits in very well with the plans of the globalists. Since the globalists have locked themselves into the Malthusian theory of surplus population and limited resources, something must be done to bring the populations in line with the limited resources. The world has 4.5-billion people but the globalists believe it must contain only 2.5-billion by the year 2000. (See *Global 2000 Report* especially volume 2). This means programs must be designed not only to prevent population increase but provide a roll back of two billion by the year 2000.

The world faces a population problem but it is not overpopulation but population distribution. The United States is actually a dying nation. We are not producing enough children to replace ourselves. The problem is compounded by controlled social pressure for families to have fewer or no children or children later in married life. Lifestyles that require both spouses to work as well as feminist programs add their part to reduced family size and population control. In addition the diverse or alternate lifestyle of homosexuality is another unobtrusive population control mechanism. Homosexual marriages do not produce children and this sexual preference is increased by recruitment.

Some sex education programs actually encourage participation in homosexual activities on the pretense of research and experimentation. It should also be a source of concern that part of the gay rights push is for adoption rights to children and foster parent programs.

The most apparent population control method of course is abortion, a national disgrace. Abortion, like tolerance toward homosexuality, is a symptom of a nation coming under judgment. The present abortion rate is 1.5-million unborn babies each year. This is larger than our standing army, so each year we are killing more than an army of our future population.

Since the Supreme Court decision that legalized the immorality of abortion there have been more than 13-million abortions in our nation, a greater loss of life than all the fatalities combined of every war in which our nation has been involved since its founding.

> *Cursed is he who accepts a fee to strike down an INNOCENT person.*
> Deuteronomy 27:25

> *Keep far from a lie, and do not kill the INNOCENT or the righteous, for I will not acquit the guilty.*
> Exodus 23:7

What could be more innocent than the unborn babies so miraculously conceived yet so unmercifully destroyed? Keep in mind that there is no such thing as a safe abortion. There is a fatality involved in each one — the baby dies. It is well worth while to read David Jeremiah's chapter on abortion in his book *Before It's Too Late.*

Is there any difference between lamp shades being made out of human skin and using abortion substance for cosmetic bases? Does it make it "right," because we are doing it instead of the Nazis?

I challenge the abortionists to consider where they would be if their mothers had believed as they do about the pregnancy that conceived them.

Beware of the infanticide against children with birth defects. You have another camel with his nose in the tent. Once a quality of life yardstick is permitted, the measure or degree of quality can become very subjective to include anyone. Remember, globalists believe Christians are insane. Could the insane become as non-persons the same as unborn babies to be exterminated? It happened in Nazi Germany.

I know the parents and the public in general are mostly unaware of how large a problem they face in trying to get the abortion/homosexual mentality out of the schools. For example, on February 25 and 26, 1982, the Training Institute of Planned Parenthood of Maryland held a workshop entitled "New Approaches to Family Life Education for School Nurses and Counselors."

Planned Parenthood is the abortion promoter throughout the nation.

This particular workshop not only indoctrinated school nurses and counselors with the usual pro-abortion push but successfully convinced many of the attendees to return to their schools and promote the acceptance of alternate lifestyles, i.e., homosexuality, as normal!

Equally compatible with the Zero Population game plan is the high suicide rate and incurable diseases, such as AIDS and herpes.

"Report is made that South Eastern Middle School has

been *selected* by Planned Parenthood of Central Pennsylvania, Inc. to pilot a sexual abuse prevention project . . ."

This item was on the agenda under new business of the South Eastern School District meeting of the Board of School Directors, January 12, 1984. I was attending this meeting on behalf of a family whose child was being "humanized" in a gifted and talented course in that middle school.

Could you imagine the outcry that would be heard if a local church had *selected* the same school — or any school — for evangelization, yet that is exactly what Planned Parenthood does — evangelizes! This is happening nationwide and will continue to happen because the majority of Christians don't want to become controversial or confrontational. If the Lord had believed that way, He would have never been sacrificed for our sins.

Man Is a Throw Away but Save the Snail Darter

Globalism is an interesting paradox. Its humanistic philosophy stresses the centrality of man over God yet fosters every imaginable method of human destruction. Individual man is expendable although he is an "evolving god," according to the New Agers.

How can you get society to accept as much carnage as exists today?

The covert objective of death education was to DE-SENSITIZE children to the phenomenon of death so that as adults they will accept 1.5-million abortions each year, participate unhesitatingly in *real* survival situations by eliminating less productive non-persons and agree to infanticide, euthanasia and suicide. In the matter of suicide the desensitizing has been so successful that suicide is the number two killer of American youth, reaching into the elementary grades for its victims.

(Organizations such as Hemlock in Pennsylvania and

Exit in England now exist to help people in their suicidal efforts).

It is a tribute to the authors, teachers and philosophy of values clarification and behavior modification that society now tolerates and practices all the abominations of the globalist zero population program.

Society as well as government school children are incessantly bombarded with survival conditioning. Beginning with pre-schoolers, children are conditioned to believe that in order to survive they must embrace particular behavioral skills — usually dog-eat-dog or look out for number one or else you won't survive.

The message taught to pupils in such school situations as death ed and survival games is that there are no rules. Society doesn't exist and the only laws are those you create for yourself, i.e., everyone for himself, a jungle. With no biblical discipline incorporated, fall out shelter, life boat or dome city survival games confront immature minds with the responsibility of valuing the quality of life of a number of classmates with the idea of eliminating those that don't measure up.

Often the bias for survival is in favor of those who possess characteristics completely opposite to the accepted American standards but very much in accord with the beliefs of humanism, e.g., homosexuality.

These survival strategies place ten elementary school children in a circle of desks which represents a life boat, fall out shelter or domed city. They are told that they have only enough supplies for seven to survive. The children must then place a value on each other and decide on three classmates to be eliminated. This conditions children to determine quality of life standards and to accept elimination of the "unfit."

The moral consequences involved are never introduced and the children are conditioned to accept these procedures and processes as normal. The individual becomes unimportant and can be sacrificed for the survival of the society. Can you see other covert motivations behind such role playing?

Euthanasia, or mercy killing, will soon achieve social acceptance. It is for the terminally ill but it doesn't take a genius to realize that the globalists also intend it for the unproductive or "useless eater" who puts a drain on the global society. The retarded, the handicapped, the mentally ill, the criminal — since man is a throw away in surplus population theory, the standard for survival could be quite high and exclude many groups lacking the appropriate quality of life to justify consumption of valuable and scarce resources. The abortion or infanticide of babies with birth defects is a big step toward all kinds of ramifications for eliminating certain populations.

A concept being discussed in the globalist writings with increasing frequency is body farming or neomorts. Whenever you have a society practicing "quality of life" the useless eater becomes a prime target for spare body parts; man is just another animal anyway in such a society.

This was horrifying when practiced by the Nazis, but our globalist society of today finds it acceptable. The bodies of people legally dead have been kept alive so body parts can be used for transplants. Some pregnant women who were to have abortions carried the child longer so the baby's vital organs could be used for transplants.

John Whitehead in his book *The Stealing of America* includes an account of a researcher keeping "alive" the heads of aborted babies for experimentation.

Cases dealing with these issues are already coming before the courts. In a Kentucky case the court decided to permit the removal of a kidney from a retarded brother to save the older brother's life but in a 1978 U.S. court case the court decided that a cousin did not have to donate bone marrow but called the refusal "morally inexcusable." (Do You Own Your Body? *The Futurist,* December 1981)

Don't forget the Zero Population advocates are aiming for 100 million surgical contraceptions each year.

The Demise Pill

In the December 1981 issue of *The Futurist* magazine, the bimonthly publication of the World Future Society, a letter discussing the demise (death) pill was featured on the Letters to the Editor page. The letter thoroughly typified the posture of the globalist toward the elderly. The writer proposed a death pill be mandated at a predetermined age to "defuse the population explosion at the end of life, as did making family planning techniques available for the beginning of life." The justification for such a pill was that no health or retirement insurance program could survive the increasing number of elderly people and something had to be done to keep the productive young people from being "inundated by people whose lives no longer hold meaning for anyone . . ."

Wisdom is with aged men,
With long life is understanding.
Job 12:12

. . . honor the aged, and you will revere your God;
I am the Lord.
Leviticus 19:32

We must learn to use some tools of the trade in order to discern the networking that exists among the globalists because it's the same cast of characters with different labels: futurists, globalists, humanists, etc. We did a little of this with the computer connection and Project Basic in Chapter 4. Begin checking the names listed in small print along the sides of organization stationary or on the editor's page.

Among the directors of *The Futurist* magazine you will find some names of interest:

★ Orville L. Freeman, president, Business International Corporation, former U.S. Secretary of Agriculture under President Kennedy. As an aside you may want to check the Fall 1983 issue of *Girl Scout Leader.* Jane C. Freeman, wife of Orville Freeman, is national president of the Girl Scouts.

This particular manual has a special section, "Global Understanding Projects," following page 20. The globalist motto "Think Globally, Act Locally" is prominently displayed and the first line reads, "Girl Scouts have always been concerned about universal problems such as hunger, illiteracy, and *depletion of natural resources.*"

Anything sound familiar? I always thought the Girl Scouts were interested in developing Christian and moral character. The global merit badges include the seven-ray rainbow of the New Age, the pagan sun burst and the Sign of the Satellite. The projects are loaded with sensitivity awareness and other behavior mod and values clarification techniques including a "World Association pin, a symbol of the international scope of the *Movement.*" The Boy Scouts are just as bad. They earn merit badges in global citizenship).

★ John W. Gardner, chairman, Independent Sector, former U.S. Secretary of *Health, Education* and *Welfare* under President Carter.

★ Glenn T. Seaborg, professor of chemistry, University of California at Berkeley, former chairman, U.S. Atomic Energy Commission under President Carter, member of the National Commission on Excellence in Education.

★ Rowen A. Wakefield, principal, Wakefield Washington Association, Inc., former vice president, Aspen Institute. (Remember that the Aspen Institute is the major advocate of humanistic studies in the United States. According to a *Sunpaper* article its members are advisors to Walter Mondale on economic policy. Mondale is a presidential candidate and former vice president under President Carter).

These men have held high positions in our government. In addition, the Wye Plantation, which is the eastern branch of the Aspen Institute, frequently hosts congressmen at its palatial estate on the Eastern Shore of Maryland where they participate in various workshops.

What concerns me is the amount of humanist philosophy that has been translated into federal policy, e.g., S. 1771 in the 1st Session of the 97th Congress and H.R. 907 in the 2nd Session of the 97th Congress which if passed would have "established in the Federal Government a *global* foresight capability with respect to natural resources, the environment, the population; to establish a national population policy; to establish an interagency Council on *Global Resources*, Environment, and *Population*, and FOR OTHER PURPOSES."

Population control as a federal policy is not that far away in our future.

Agriculture will be the major tool used by the globalists to convince people that a surplus population — drawing on an inadequate food supply — exists.

Global 2000

CHAPTER 7

Crisis Management

Do not be deceived, God is not mocked; for whatever a man sows, this he will also reap.
Galatians 6:7

How do the globalists get us to do what they want us to do? If you read the title to this chapter, you know the answer. The process is effective and ongoing and everyone has participated at some time in a crisis management situation.

Crisis management makes you willing to sit in gas lines for hours, wasting gas to get a ration of gas, when there is no petroleum shortage. Ten years ago if anyone had told you that you would sit in line for gas and pay over a dollar per gallon, you would have thought they were crazy. In less than ten years we have sat in lines twice and we pay over a dollar a gallon for gas — this is crisis management. It puts you in a position where you are willing to do what they want you to do for you to get what you want.

There is no energy crisis and never was. (See *The Energy Non Crisis* by Lindsey Williams, chaplain for the Alaskan pipeline). There is so much oil that OPEC can hardly keep itself together because of oil surpluses. Mexico, now a major oil producer, is on the verge of economic collapse because oil just isn't that important. The Alaskan oil fields are so vast they must be kept out of production or the oil industry would collapse.

How do you take an oil glut and create gas lines at filling stations?

First, you reduce the number of retail outlets to minimize the number of commercial suppliers. The relics of this effort are symbolized by the numerous unoccupied gas stations on many street corners. Remember when the major oil companies put all their independent distributors out of business by calling their loans and cutting their fuel allotments?

Second, you reduce production and what you have you withhold from distribution. Remember the news stories about great supplies of oil being found in every pipe line, storage tank, and oil tankers just waiting to be unloaded?

Third, you increase foreign exports of petroleum because foreign countries pay much higher prices for it and that keeps the fuel off the domestic market. This was the game plan used for creating the fuel crisis.

I believe agriculture and food supply will be the next national crisis management scam. Famine can be orchestrated just as other catastrophes. It will convince people that there is a surplus population drawing on an inadequate food supply as well as help roll back population due to starvation.

Unfortunately for our country and the rest of the world we have had a number of men in key agricultural positions in government who are subscribers to globalism.

The Hunger Project, begun by EST, collects and spends millions on advertising that hunger exists in the world but not a cent is spent on food for the hungry.

Werner Earhart, the founder and mover of EST, was closely allied with Planetary Citizen and globalist Buckminster Fuller, inventor of the geodesic dome. Fuller considered nationalism (love of country) the blood clot of the world's circulatory system.

Why famine?

First, many food chains have considerably reduced their retail outlets — after they eliminated most independent grocers.

Second, we have committed ourselves to huge, long-term food or grain sales to foreign countries, mainly enemy communist nations.

Third, food production is being seriously curtailed. Food supply is controlled by farmers and farmers are controlled by bankers. Because of high interest rates many farmers have been forced into receivership. The same bankers that created the high interest rates now own the farms.

Large bankers as well as oil and energy industrialists are global architects.

For example, a series of articles in the business section of the *Baltimore Sun* newspaper noted that Citibank raised its prime interest rate to 16½ percent, reversing a downward trend which had been triggering a recovery. Following is the comment some other bankers made:

"Some bankers said that they feared that a new surge in short-term interest rates could throw many businesses into bankruptcy and some question whether market conditions justify this large increase in the prime rate at this time."

In the next paragraph the article states that stock market prices tumbled. Citibank could care less. Bankruptcy is crisis management.

Crisis management puts the masses in a situation

where they do not care about long-range consequences because they are too concerned about the tyranny of the immediate. The globalists happily provide their solutions to the problems they have created. Since they control the government, their solutions are usually government programs: "We'll take care of you. We'll provide your needs." We accept their solutions rather than go through the hassle of fighting the system. Look at the IRS (Infernal — my spelling — Revenue Service). We accept all kinds of burdensome taxes and regulations just to escape an IRS hassle. Wasn't the American Revolution fought over such issues?

Can unemployment be a form of crisis management? In Harford County, Maryland, where I live there are now six thousand people unemployed. Are they worried about globalism? Are they interested in what Bill Bowen has to say about one world government? They are worried about where they are going to get enough money for their house payments and how they can keep their family fed and clothed. The globalists changed these people's concerns about where the family will spend its vacation or how much offering they can give on Sunday to what they must do and need to do to *survive*. The unemployment crisis put all of them on government assistance of one kind or another. It put a lot of adults back into school for retraining. It destabilized a lot of families due to economic stress. It was all because the globalists decided we must become an automated informational society so they began dismantling our industry.

Can the anti-industry stance of the globalists explain why President Reagan's defense programs had so much trouble in Congress? Military buildup requires heavy industry. Heavy industry uses natural resources in large quantities and also is labor intensive. It provides a lot of jobs and stability. This is crisis management.

Once some examples are pointed out, it is easy to see more and more occasions where crisis management has been used on us as a nation.

As a final example for us to consider at this time, I want you to recall the minute books of the Carnegie Endowment directors and their conclusion that war effects the greatest amount of change on the largest number of people. (See Chapter 3). Don't be confused by the seeming contradiction of purpose when the globalists are found sponsoring both war and peace efforts. Control is the objective and conflict is the method. Pitting NEA against PEA, KKK against NAACP, etc. is conflict which permits control or manipulation by the globalists.

The globalist peace movement is not interested in peace but in disarmament. Disarmament permits industrial dismantling which creates unemployment. Unemployment facilitates crisis management.

Disarmament also will force the surrender of the United States, basically the only remaining free enterprise economy, to the militarily superior socialist governments, thus initiating the one world or globalist government. Think back to the beginning of this page. If you don't have a war as a vehicle of change and control, what is the next best thing? Terrorism!

Terrorist activity is as much a part of the globalist program as drugs, mind control, sex ed, New Age and Eastern cults, Hunger Projects, and war. Notice where most of the terrorist revolutions and guerrilla wars occur: the most densely populated areas — the loss of life is running in the millions — and the areas that produce more food, oil and resources than needed; e.g., Southeast Asia and the Middle East, El Salvador, Nicaragua and Central America in general. Terrorist activity reduces production and consumption of the areas' resources, especially food, and replaces them with disease, death, destruction, famine and DESPAIR. Despair is a major force in crisis management.

Although globalism is atheistic, it isn't an accident that globalists support the forces of liberation theology. Control is the objective anyway: the greater the conflict, the greater the change and the greater the control.

The proponents of liberation theology collaborate with the socialists in overthrowing conservative, rightist governments. One edition of the Catholic magazine, *The New Covenant*, was largely dedicated to pointing out that the priests and nuns who had collaborated with the revolutionaries in Nicaragua were finding themselves divested of power and rights and were being imprisoned or executed. Belatedly, the testimony of these priests and nuns was that cooperation with atheism in the form of socialism just doesn't work. This revelation is coming too late in Nicaragua but the same mistake is being repeated in El Salvador and the other Latin American states. Terrorism is crisis management.

Christians should remember:

We are afflicted in every way, but not crushed; persecuted, but not forsaken, struck down, but not destroyed...
                    2 Corinthians 4:8,9

CHAPTER 8

Even More About
Public Enemy No. 1

As an education student at the Johns Hopkins University (BA, MEd, PhD equivalent), I studied Plato, Hegel, Pestalozzi, Mann and Dewey. It is difficult to imagine anyone successfully completing the program without a thorough familiarity with the philosophy of these men and their influence on education in America.

Looking back it is interesting to recall that nearly every education student rejected these philosophies as impractical or merely curious hypotheses, yet no one among us ever asked (1) why should we spend so much time on theorists who obviously were incompatible with mainstream America, and (2) why were the concepts of these men always the ones promoted and eventually implemented despite the vast indifference or vocal annoyance on the part of classroom teachers?

These philosophies were persistently incorporated and their methods infused into educational programs. Evidently we mistakenly believed that we would continue to have the option of using them or ignoring them. Presently there is no such option.

For the same reasons that school children accept the education we offer them, teachers accept the programs and materials presented and required of them: the authority of the instructor or administrator and the credibility of the educational establishment. Our children submit to sex ed, values clarification, death ed and behavior mod because they think that's what we as parents want them to learn. They may even believe that the education they are getting is the same as Mom and Dad got or they may be too embarrassed even to discuss what they are learning with their parents.

Origins of the Specious — The Ancients

In my opinion the United States is the only nation left in the world today which was founded for godly purposes. (The Promised Land of the Hebrews predates our nation but disappeared in 70 A.D. The present Israel, although in God's purpose, was founded for various reasons, none of which were necessarily godly).

Between the landing of the Pilgrims at Plymouth Rock and the American Revolution our Christian resolve had waned but God still saw fit to provide us with leaders who were strong in their faith. Even those leaders who professed atheism or deism were very familiar with scripture and understood the wisdom of its teachings. Consequently most of their policies were based on biblical principles or greatly influenced by them.

The Constitution they wrote and the republic it established are truly gifts from God to His people who are called by His name. We fail to recognize and appreciate this because of our ignorance of the Constitution and the Bible, thanks to the efforts of the public school system and the liberal church. We have been poor stewards of the bounty God promised to His people and which He has poured out upon us.

Plato in his *Republic* imagined an ideal state. It would have a government under the authority of philosophers (teachers of his day) who would rule as kings and possess great wisdom. Their purpose would be to reveal "truth" and bring a general welfare into being. The state would be populated by the masses which would consist of laborers and craftsmen with minimal education or vocational training, like state-owned slaves. To insure obedience to the government the family unit would be abolished and the children would be raised by the state. To secure the stability of the government — since force might be needed to accomplish its goals — there would be a military class to protect the government and its ruling elite and preserve peace among the populace.

If you looked behind the camouflage, this is just about where public education is heading today. As each generation becomes less knowledgeable about the biblical and constitutional bases of our government the easier it becomes for philosopher-tyrants to create such a police state as Plato's *Republic*.

As William Penn, proprietor and founder of Pennsylvania, so aptly stated, "You can either believe in God or be ruled by Tyrants."

Rousseau envisioned for France such a government as Plato described and focused on the education of children and the rewriting of history as a way of bringing it into existence. Rousseau's education involved no discipline or restraints for children except those freely arrived at by the child. Sounds like Sidney Simon's values clarification, doesn't it?

On May 1, 1776, in Bavaria, Professor Adam Weishaupt started an Illuminati cell at Ingolstadt University where he occupied the chair of Canon Law. Weishaupt was a

Jew who had studied to become a Jesuit but never joined the order.

Illuminism is believed to have originated in Italy, possibly an outgrowth of Gnosticism which put reason above faith, indulged in immorality and practiced spiritualism. By 1492 Illuminism was very prominent in Spain although regarded as a cult. In 1527 Ignatius Loyola, who became the founder of the Jesuit order in 1541, was arrested in Spain for Illuminist and Gnostic activity but not convicted. (See Gerald Winrod, *Adam Weishaupt,* Emmissary Publications, 1937, pp. 12 and 26. Also Stan Deyo, *The Cosmic Conspiracy,* WATT, 1978, p. 65). The communist celebration — May 1 — is the commemoration of Weishaupt's founding of the Illuminati.

Although the Illuminati may no longer exist in name, the top echelons of both the Jesuits and the Masons — especially the European Masons — are still believed to be committed to the beliefs of Weishaupt. Weishaupt's objective was to take over the Masonic Orders in Europe and use them to foment a world revolution. (Winrod, pp. 18 and 23). In time he managed to bring the other Illuminati — the Alumbrados in Spain which were under the Jesuits and Franciscans and the Guerinet among the young noblemen in France — under his aegis as well as most other occult activities. (See Deyo, p. 65).

I doubt if the rank and file of either order have any idea of the sinister intentions of some of their leaders any more than the parents and teachers knew about the hidden agenda of policy makers in public education. Knowing the truth will set us free but our resistance to truth is often the most difficult obstacle to overcome.

Keep in mind that Jesuits were created to serve as the army of the Roman Catholic Church. Their purpose was to check and eliminate Protestantism. The Jesuit constitution states that the end justifies the means and any moral law may be broken to promote the Church and attack Protestantism. (Winrod, pp. 29, 30)

The Jesuits also became the educators and were able to shape the ideas of their pupils according to Jesuit purposes.

Weishaupt's own activities reflect the influence of the fierce militaristic training as well as his propensity for the occult which he acquired from his association with Kolmer, a Cabalist Jew from Egypt and practitioner of Satanism. (Winrod, p. 18)

Abbe' Barruel, a contemporary of Weishaupt, described the techniques of Weishaupt's "values clarification and behavior modification" (my terminology) in his book *Anti-Christian Conspiracy*. In summary: it always began with corruption of morals in small doses which gradually increased. The youth were told that marriage was not necessary, that children were not beholden to their fathers and that vengeance was incompatible with a loving God so there was no hell to fear. To the lodge life meant nothing and it assumed the power of life and death decisions. To control things they began the method still used in Russia today, "Everybody is a spy spying on a spy." (Today it's MBO or PPBS).

Winrod quotes the Marquis de Luchet just before the French Revolution as saying, "This society (the Illuminati) aims at governing the world. Its object is universal domination."

The French Revolution was based on the propaganda that the poor could not help themselves, the rich must be suppressed, class war would bring about an ideal state and a dictatorship of the proletariat should rule. Reason was the religion of man instead of Christianity and a prostitute was worshipped as the Goddess of Reason in the Cathedral of Notre Dame.

Weishaupt was called the Patriarch of the Jacobins by the French Illuminized Masons. It was the Jacobins that led the French into the Reign of Terror blood bath. Today we have the communists continuing the blood bath tradition.

The Russian Revolution was justified with the same reasons as the French Revolution. It shouldn't surprise us that the same arguments are used today in America by the progressive educrats, who control public education, and the liberal left to justify their programs.

Weishaupt's program for world revolution had six fundamental propositions:
   1) Abolition of all ordered government
   2) Abolition of inheritance
   3) Abolition of private property
   4) Abolition of patriotism to national states
   5) Abolition of family, sex laws and moral codes
   6) Abolition of religion based on faith in God

"Communism abolished eternal truths, it abolishes all religion, and all morality . . . it therefore acts in contradiction to all past historical experience." For the word "communism" you could substitute Illuminism, humanism, progressive education or values clarification and the rest of the sentence could remain unchanged and still be correct. The quote, however, is from *The Communist Manifesto*. (Karl Marx, *The Communist Manifesto*, American Opinion Press, 1974, p. 24).

What plans did Karl Marx have for advanced countries such as America?
   1) Abolition of property in land and application of all rents of land to public purposes. (This is coming through taxes and zoning codes).
   2) A heavy progressive or graduated income tax. (Have you heard of the IRS?)
   3) Abolition of all right of inheritance. (Inheritance tax — rich excluded via foundations).
   4) Confiscation of property of all emigrants (those who flee the country) and rebels. (Christian dissidents perhaps?)

5) Centralization of the means of communication and transport in the hands of the State. (After the prices for gas and telephone service go up due to deregulation and anti trust suits (AT&T), we will beg the government for this).

6) Extension of factories and instruments of production owned by the State, the bringing into cultivation of waste lands and the improvement of the soil generally in accordance with a common plan. (Soil bank, EPA, government subsidies, price supports, etc.).

7) Equal liability of all to labor. Establishment of industrial armies, especially for agriculture. (Workmen's compensation, free enterprise zones, "required, voluntary" community service).

8) Combination of agriculture with manufacturing industries; gradual abolition of the distinction between town and country by a more equitable distribution of population over the country. (Consolidation by bank foreclosures and Newstates planned for 1987).

9) Free education for all children in public schools. Abolition of children's factory labor in its present form. Combination of education with industrial production. (Community schools, free enterprise zones and computer hookup to global curriculum).

We've come a long way, baby, from 1776 and 1787.

There are too many similarities — in beliefs and practices, between Illuminism, communism, progressive education — and the current drift of our government — to be coincidental. Even the practice of assuming different names, e.g., Weishaupt's Illuminati name was Spartacus.

It is interesting that the Red communists in the early days of the Russian Revolution called themselves Spartacusts and not communists. (Winrod, p. 48)

Lenin's real name was Zederbaum, Trotsky's was Bronstein, Litvinoff's was Finklestein and Rodak's was Sobelsohn. The Sabbath was destroyed in both the French and

Russian Revolutions. It is presently being destroyed in America by the repeal of Blue Laws. Atheism became the state religion in France and Russia, humanism in America.

Weishaupt was successful because he was able to combine the permissiveness of Rousseau's education for change with the militant zeal of the Jesuits, the secrecy of the Masons, and the wealth and influence of powerful families such as the Rothschilds. (See Count Egon Caesar Corti, *The Rise of the House of Rothschild*, Western Islands, 1972, Introduction). Humanism and communism advance in America because wealthy families and their foundations fund these movements.

Johann Fichte was another German professor who influenced American education. Like Rousseau he believed pupils should not be taught to read until late in life, if at all; that the teachers were the *real parents*; and that educators should be the rulers of the state.

In his book *The Impact of Science on Society* socialist Bertrand Russell summarized Fichte's intent as "education should aim at destroying free will so that after pupils are thus schooled they will be incapable throughout the rest of their lives of thinking or acting otherwise than as their school masters would have wished."

The concept of operant conditioning in education has a long history. Until America established the present compulsory public school system it was able to escape most of these perverse influences.

George Hegel was another significant influence on American education. He believed war kept a government strong and he is famous for the statement, "The State is God." Since there were many who held that the state was superior to the individual, it is easy to see where the philosophical roots of Prussian and Nazi militarism ori-

Education

ginated. That thinking parallels the idea in American education that the children belong to the government.

Johann Herbart's contribution to American education today lingers in the "enrichment" curricula and education methodology. While a student at Jena University he became closely associated with Johann Herder (Damascus pontifex in the Illuminati), Johann Goethe (Abaris in the Illuminati), and Johann Fichte, who was a close friend of Goethe. Herbart later spent three years with Pestalozzi (Alfred in the Illuminati) at Interlaken in Switzerland. Obviously the Illuminati exerted considerable influence on Herbart through his friends. He even wrote a book about Pestalozzi and his education theories. The Illuminati wanted world domination by any means and was anti-Christian. (See Anthony Sutton, *How the Order Controls Education,* Research Publications, 1983, p. 28).

The Origin of the Specious — The Modernists

It seems farfetched to us today that educational theorists in a far-off country could have such influence on the American educational system. But at the time the public school system in America was developing the above were the men whose ideas were being implemented in American education. The evidence is irrefutable that many of their ideas are in our educational system today. Educrats today, having accomplished their goals, are now studying the Chinese educational system and soon our schools will be mirroring theirs.

Wilhelm Wundt, a philosophy professor at Berlin University, pioneered experimental psychology. He was intrigued by the social theories of Hegel and Herbart. He believed that man, being animalistic — as Charles Darwin theorized — was but a combined product of all his sensations and stimuli. He also set up the first experimental psychology laboratory to measure human stimuli responses.

American scholars in education and psychology went to Europe to study under Wundt then returned and set up education and psychology departments in American colleges. What they brought back were Hegel and Herbart theories mixed with Wundt's beliefs: man was just an animal subject to the state and influenced by experience or stimuli and that "morality" was whatever was good for society.

Three of the most important American educators went to Germany to study at the Berlin University while Hegelian philosophy was unchallenged and all-pervasive. (Two of these men studied directly under Wundt). They were Timothy Dwight who became president of Yale University, Daniel Gilman who became the first president of the University of California, the first president of the Johns Hopkins University (modeled on German scholarship), and then president of the Carnegie Institute; and Andrew Dickson White who became the first president of Cornell University and first president of the American Historical Association.

G. Stanley Hall was also among Wundt's American students. Later he was hired by Antioch College to take Horace Mann's place. (Mann was the promoter of looksay reading and first president of Antioch).

Hall later returned to Leipzig and was the first of dozens of Americans to receive a Ph.D. in psychology under Wundt. On his return to the United States he was employed by Gilman as professor of philosophy and pedagogy (education) at The Hopkins. Politically Hall leaned toward Marxism. (Sutton, p. 42) This was the beginning of the "modern" educational movement including the parapsychology now being employed.

John Dewey was one of the first Ph.D.s to study under

experimental psychologist G. Stanley Hall and Hegelian philosopher George S. Morris at The Hopkins. Afterwards Dewey went to the University of Michigan as a philosophy professor. Later he moved to the University of Chicago and founded the School of Education with Rockefeller money. Next he went to Columbia and set up the Teachers College.

Dewey's education was state centered: the value of education is to teach that the state is absolute. Freedom was in obedience to the state, a sense of community and collective identity in a world society.

He organized the leftist American Association of University Professors. In 1941 he was president of the League for Industrial Democracy (LID) which had been organized in 1905 as the Intercollegiate SOCIALIST Society "to promote an interest in socialism among college men and women."

The organization advocated "education for the new social order based on production for use and not for profit." (See Erminie K. Wright, *The Conquest of Democracy*, Educational Research Bureau, p. 4. This little booklet preserved the original minutes and documents of the NEA and their reports for 1933, 1934 and 1935 when the "new society" educators were taking over the American education system).

Dewey was also an admirer of pioneer Fabian socialist James Harvey Robinson who taught history at Columbia University. Robinson believed that materials used in the classroom should be carefully selected to promote socialism. He also rewrote history books to provide a socialist slant, a new history.

Colonel Francis W. Parker also influenced Dewey and stressed that children should be free from adult tyranny and ridiculed discipline. He helped eliminate corporal punishment from the schools and promoted the idea of the changing "functional" curriculum.

Dewey served on the NEA Committee on Social-Economic Goals of America (1931). Its report stated, "A national ideal will no longer suffice in itself ... The chief instrumentality to mold public opinion... is education ..." (Wright, p. 5)

The humanist Horace Mann, who was a major creator of our public school system, possessed some curious educational qualifications. His teacher, Samuel Barrett, described him as an idiot in arithmetic, unable to recite the multiplication tables or tell time by a clock. For six months he would be an earnest teacher but for the other six months he was in "a state of beastly drunkeness (sic) ..." Mann wanted a universal education system free of religion — a goal still cherished by public education today. (Sutton, p. 22)

I believe you can go into most classrooms today and the teacher will know something about John Dewey and even recognize the names of Pestalozzi and Mann. If you mention the Illuminati, they probably will think you are talking about an Italian light bulb manufacturer. Despite the fact that they are completely antithetical to the foundations of our country, it is amazing how much of the philosophies of Weishaupt, the other German theorists and even Plato have been preserved to this day in American education.

Willard E. Givens gave a report for the American Association of School Administrators (AASA) at the 1934 NEA convention called "Education for the New America" that said, "A dying *laissez-faire* must be completely destroyed ... Attitudes are the desirable objectives ... thinking must be international in scope ... these demands will make education cost more ..." (Wright, p. 7) Givens became the executive secretary of the NEA the next year, 1935, and in that year created the Educational Policies Commission funded by the Rockefeller-endowed General Education Board.

George S. Counts of Columbia served with Givens on the Commission. Counts was very vocal in his expression of admiration for the "great collectivist experiment in Russia" and advocated a "coordinated, planned, and SOCIALIZED economy." He was associate director of the International Institute at Columbia Teachers College (Rockefeller funded), served on the board of directors of the League for Industrial Democracy (Intercollegiate Socialist League until 1921) and a member of the ACLU. Counts' pamphlet "The Soviet Challenge to America" is listed in the Communist Leaders Handbook for recommended reading. (Wormser, pp. 145 and 153; Wright p. 10)

Counts' chairmanship and participation in education associations and on committees made him a major contributor to using the public schools as the vehicle to socialize America.

James B. Conant, president of Harvard University and a member of the Council on Foreign Relations, also served on the Commission. It was his suggestion that Citizens Committees of prominent local citizens be used to justify (unwittingly) the costly school consolidation programs, paving the way for the "Better Schools" project. Conant toured the nation's school districts with the consolidation gospel. This program in which we are still trapped (the education cluster or park) provides local communities with fixed, burgeoning bonded debts, provides tax-exempt investments for moneyed interests and removes the child from the influence of the parent and neighborhood for long hours each day.

Sidney B. Hall, superintendent of public instruction for Virginia (1930-1941) also served on the Commission. Hall made many changes in the Virginia education program which for years had been a model for other systems. He instituted the core curriculum in place of required subjects and while the pupils wallowed in "challenging social problems" they learned to "cooperate rather than compete."

In 1931 he started the Virginia Plan to bring the state's educational system in line with George Counts' program, "Dare the Schools Build a NEW SOCIAL ORDER?" The Rockefeller Foundation's General Education Board provided a grant for counselors to help high school principals put the new programs in place. They were then monitored by "carefully chosen" supervisors, counselors and directors of instruction. Teachers were no longer professionals but regimented, unionized laborers.

Edmund E. Day, president of Cornell University, was on the Commission. He previously had been the Director of Social Sciences of the Rockefeller Foundation. In his 1939 address to the NEA convention he made clear his belief that the purpose of schools is to bring about a new social order. (See Edmund E. Day, "How Can Our Schools Contribute to a Better Social Order?" and Wright, p. 17).

To guarantee nationwide incorporation of these policies for a new socialist social order, White House conferences were held and reluctant delegates were made "part of the problem" by group dynamics methods which submerged their concerns beneath majority *consensus*. The "Better Schools" program, the Marshall Plan for education, began its sweep across the country while the National Citizens Commission for the Public Schools began a media blitz under the leadership of eight members of the "Invisible Government," the Council on Foreign Relations.

A case book was published by the Commission (NEA) and the AASP, entitled *Learning the Ways of Democracy*. It included outlines, subject matter and techniques such as integrated courses, class discussions, cooperative entertainment through drama, regimented sports and guidance counseling. The Preamble presented an entirely alien definition of "social welfare," as the meaning of the term "general welfare."

It Will Never Happen Here

How successful has educational brainwashing been? *National Education Program,* November 1981, reproduced a survey done by *U.S. News and World Report* of high school and college students. Colleges such as Northwestern, Purdue and Wisconsin participated. These are highly competitive and academic schools. Here are some of the results:

★ 61 percent of the students said the *profit incentive* wasn't necessary to the survival of *free enterprise.* (They didn't realize that profit incentive *is* the center of free enterprise).

★ 62 percent thought a worker should *not produce* all he can. (They didn't realize this practice would push production cost up and reduce the standard of living).

★ 62 percent said the government has the responsibility to *provide jobs.* (Every job requires invested capital. To provide jobs government taxation would exhaust private funds).

★ 56 percent believed there should be *close* government *regulations* of all business. (Government regulation of business is largely responsible for today's economic problems).

★ 53 percent believed in government ownership of banks, railroads and steel companies. (This would be socialism).

How successful has socialistic education been in America? These students didn't know anything about free enterprise but more than half believed in socialism.

The Pro-Family Forum *Alert,* February 1984, reproduced an article from January 21, 1984, *Dallas Morning News*, which said:

"The school board of Berkeley, California, has decided not to require the Pledge of Allegiance in public schools. The Berkeley City Council had previously voted not to salute the flag before meetings, and many of the schools had already discontinued flying flags.

"The school board will design a substitute optional pledge urging world peace, a pledge which will express 'hope for a just and peaceful society,' according to school spokeswoman Beth Mesmick.

" 'We have a peace committee that will work with the children to come up with their own pledge,' explained board member Barbara Lubin. She said: 'In terms of pledging allegiance to a flag, we will never make a child in this city pledge allegiance to anything. One Nation Under God — I don't believe it. I haven't saluted the flag in 10 years and I think I'm a good citizen.' "

During one of my presentations someone in the audience asked me how I reconcile the scriptural teaching "love thine enemies" with my position. I said I do love MY enemies, but the Lord didn't ask me to love HIS enemies.

Do I not hate those who hate thee, O Lord?
And do I not loathe those who rise up against Thee?
I hate them with the utmost hatred;
They have become my enemies.
　　　　　　Psalm 139:21,22

The Origin of the Specious — The Global New Age

The year 1987 will be the bicentennial of our Constitution. Kingman Brewster in his article in *Foreign Affairs*, April 1972, called for a Declaration of Interdependence in 1976 and a global constitutional convention that "might save the peoples of nations by making them into a world community capable of survival." (*Freemen Digest,* May 1978, p. 6 or *Foreign Affairs,* p. 415) In 1976 Dr. Henry Steele Commager's Declaration of Interdependence, which he wrote for the World Affairs Council of Philadelphia, was publicly signed by many members of our Congress in Independence Hall in Philadelphia.

We are now only two votes away from calling for a Constitutional Convention. Now that our one world moneyed interests have submerged us in debt there is a clamor for a balanced budget amendment coupled with school prayer and abortion amendments. What you will get is a runaway convention. There won't be a Washington or Madison or Franklin at this convention. You will have Ted Kennedy, Charles Mathias, Walter Mondale, Birch Bayh and similar political views. What will come out of this will be an ERA, world government and human rights document which will establish the Fabian socialism and redistribution of American wealth the one worlders have been planning.

Project 87 — currently in the public schools — is intended to celebrate the bicentennial of the Constitution. It is funded by grants from: the Andrew W. Mellon Foundation, the Rockefeller Foundation, the Ford Foundation, the National Endowment for the Humanities, the Lilly Endowment and the William and Flora Hewlett Foundation. This alone should give you a hint of what this program will end up teaching regardless of the good-sounding titles.

The Advisory Board is saturated with representatives from organizations that aren't inspirations for patriotism: Birch Bayh, Ted Kennedy, Charles Mathias, the former vice chair of the Commission on Civil Rights, the president of Columbia Teachers College, former Secretary of Education Shirley Hufstedler, a Columbia University jurisprudence professor, a University of Chicago law professor, the president of the Brookings Institute and others. The joint committee is as bad.

The National Endowment for the Humanities (NEH) and some thirty-plus state affiliates are using the Project '87 to "raise questions which are central to the humanities — who we are, what we are, whether there was some PURPOSE (emphasis added) behind our constitutional structure." The National Urban League, Inc. has joined the celebration. The League of Women Voters, with an NEH grant, is preparing an answer to Dr. Henry Steele Commager's rhetorical question: can an 18th-century constitution rooted in 17th-century ideas adequately meet the problems of the 20th and 21st centuries? Their answer, entitled *The Federalist Papers, Re-examined*, was designed as a "citizen" education effort.

Interdependence activities were coordinated by the State Department, the U.S. Information Agency (USIA) and the Smithsonian Institute. "Knowledge 2000" was the name of the symposia held during the International World Congress on Philosophy of Law and Social Philosophy. A global congress on "Education: The Link for Human Understanding" was held in Washington, D.C. for former Fulbright scholars, America's counterpart to the Rhodes Scholars — both are dedicated to global interdependence.

A model lesson during the symposia on George Washington and his decision to lead the Virginia delegation at the Constitutional Convention is premised on the usual affective education — "decision making. . . clarify, analyze, and make decisions." The pupils are to delve into "values" and whether Washington's decisions were "fair" in light of "the needs and wants of the community." (See *this Constitution*, Project '87, p. 21).

The bottom line with Project '87 is to prepare school children to want a new Constitutional Convention that will replace the present "outdated" one.

A Nation At Risk, the National Commission on Excellence in Education, has discovered that education in America is a "sea of mediocrity." It cost the taxpayers over $700,000 just to learn this. The rest of us already knew it. Create a problem, advertise the problem, provide a solution.

This Commission report is business as usual. It is a call for acceptance of a global perspective and the New Age. It states that "the world is indeed a global village," that we must survive in an "information age," that education is to be cradle-to-grave and the anarchy of "pluralism" is something to which we must accommodate ourselves.

The report said:

"The people of the United States need to know that individuals in our society who do not possess the levels of skill, literacy, and training essential to this NEW ERA (emphasis added) will be effectively *disenfranchised* . . . from the chance to participate in our national life." (See *A Nation At Risk,* p. 7).

When you are disenfranchised you lose your citizenship. I believe that is exactly what the Commission intends. You either achieve in the New Age or you become a slave of the state and are told what to do, when and where to do it. The Commission report calls for permissive, values-free education, parent retraining, merger of private enterprise and schools, longer days, longer school years, and millions of dollars more.

As I've said before it does not take a lot of time and money to educate a child. Church schools do a superior job for about one-third the cost of public education — and in less time. The "hidden agenda" is what takes so much time and costs so much. More money is needed in the public education sector to pay for longer school days, extended school years, more privacy-invading guidance counseling and more opportunities to bring the child under the control of the state and alienated from the parents. We should keep in mind that nowhere in the

Constitution does the federal government have the right to interfere in education. Education is not even mentioned in the document and federal government involvement is completely out of bounds.

Who are some of the members of the National Commission on Excellence?

The chairman is David P. Gardner president of the University of Utah and president-elect of the University of California. He is a close associate of Secretary Terrell Bell who is very much into computer education and a national curriculum. Others include Anne Campbell, former Nebraska State Commissioner of Education — Nebraska is where the ministers are being arrested and jailed for operating church schools; Margaret Sanger Marston, board member of Planned Parenthood and granddaughter of Margaret Sanger, founder of Planned Parenthood; Glenn T. Seaborg, director of *The Futurist* magazine, World Future Society, Professor of Chemistry at University of California; and A. Bartlett Giamatti, president of Yale who in his address to the freshman class of 1981 branded all Americans who think like the Moral Majority as a threat to the nation.

Values Education: Character Objectives and Citizenship Computerized

On April 10, 1978, the first Values Education Commission in America was created by the Maryland General Assembly — on the last day of the session. It would seem appropriate to celebrate. The great sadness is that if the basic premise of values education is wrong then the entire structure is faulty. (Sandy McKasson wrote an incisive essay on this very subject for *TRACS* in 1982 entitled "Developing A Christian Philosophy of Education." Everyone connected with Christian education should read this article).

The Maryland state attorney general said that it was

permissible to teach values as long as no religious beliefs or traditions were involved. Since American values are based on Christian teaching, how can a values program be developed with such a limitation? It doesn't matter, because the Commission is just a part of the three-step conflict-resolution ploy.

The Commission's report will become the model for other states.

The chairman was Richard Schifter. He was a member of the Coalition for a Democratic Majority, appointed by President Reagan to the Human Rights Commission in Geneva, and for 20 years had been appointed to the State Board of Education. He was president of the State Board of Education for the last four years he served.

While he was on the Board moral relativism and privacy-invasion curriculum was developed. Chronological history was abandoned. A state superintendent of schools, who did not legally qualify for the position, was hired. By-law mandate was passed. Counselors received confidentiality rights. Teenagers could receive abortions, treatment of venereal disease, birth control information and contraceptives without the knowledge or consent of their parents. Sex ed was mandated, drug ed was taught, drug use became epidemic and Project Basic was started. (See *Watch*, Vol. 4, No. 2, May 1982, p. 4).

The Coalition for a Democratic Majority called "for the establishment of a stable and viable international order," redistribution of wealth and other humanist ideals. (See *Washington Post*, December 2, 1972).

Other Coalition members were United Nations Ambassador Jeanne Kirkpatrick, Paul Kurtz, editor of *The Humanist Manifesto II* and the *Humanist* magazine, Patricia Harris, former HEW head and Schifter's law partner, Irvin Kovens, who had been recently released from prison for his involvement in the scandal in Maryland involving former Governor Marvin Mandel.

Vice chair was Mary Ann Kirk, who is the vice chair of

the Religious Heritage of America (RHA) which is lead by Clement Stone. She and Stone are also on the board of Center for Citizenship Education (CCE) along with Sargent Shriver and Planetary Citizen Norman Cousins. Clement Stone is also involved with the NEA and PTA. (See *Prince George's Journal,* April 11, 1983, p. A7).

Jack Epstein, Professor of Education at Towson State University (formerly Towson Teachers College) and the Johns Hopkins University, is another member. Epstein arranges the humanistic values clarification workshops for Sidney Simon (See *Sunpapers,* August 25, 1981).

Still another is Dr. Toni Parker, a Commission member who participated in the Sidney Simon workshop and collected the fees and defended Simon when he came under criticism. (*Op. cit*)

Kitty Shoap was a Commission member and was president of the Maryland Congress of PTAs when that group lobbied against citizen input in the selection of curriculum material.

Jeanne Kirkpatrick was a commissioner until appointed as U.S. Ambassador to the United Nations. Another member is Ernest Lefever who had his appointment to the State Department rejected by the Senate. Kirkpatrick and Lefever are involved with the committee developing the new Maryland State Social Studies Program. (*P.G. Journal,* April 11, 1983)

The point of all this is to illustrate that we must go beyond the labels of programs that only sound good. What has been demonstrated about the Values Commission will be true of other programs. On the surface the objectives and values appear acceptable, but the implementation will be a different story. The values education approaches in the back of the report are from Lawrence Kolhberg and Sidney Simon — business as usual.

The same voices we hear now with the solution to the falling SAT scores, etc., — whether it be Project'87, Values

Commission, or *A Nation At Risk* — are the same people who twenty and thirty years ago caused the present problems. What we now have in education is exactly what they programmed the public schools to create.

When the sputnik episode occurred, a hue and cry went up that millions must be poured into education to correct the paucity of science and math instruction and teachers. So we dumped millions into education but did we solve the problem? Today we are getting a rerun. Education got worse, we still have a scarcity of science and math students and teachers, but we are millions in debt. It's going to be no different this time — business as usual but more millions in debt.

North Carolina 2000 and Tuition Tax Credits

The North Carolina 2000 report to Governor James Hunt is of concern to every American citizen. If this program is implemented it will create the first socialist state in the union. Without citizen approval — as a matter of fact despite their violent disapproval — some of its educational recommendations are already being put in place. The school day and school year is being extended. Preschool day care would be licensed. Teacher certification would be changed. Skill training — and we can guess what else — would be accentuated. Higher education may force small private colleges into other fields.

In a private interview Hunt said that when the various pieces are in place, the result will be revolutionary for the state's public schools. It's hard to see the long-range impact of some of the disconnected programs but there is a pattern emerging. Thinking now turns to . . . pulling together . . . a public school kindergarten program beginning at AGE TWO. (*Winston-Salem Sentinel,* August 17, 1978)

Russia has a very comparable program. (*Los Angeles Times,* November 9, 1978, "U.S. Educators Study Soviet

Child Care")
   North Carolina citizens have been greatly concerned by the N.C. 2000 Commission's frequent referral to the *Futurist* magazine as a source for planning and discussion. One such article dealt with the Eskimo custom of the elderly seeking death as a "social duty." Another *Futurist* magazine article was on licensing and certifying of parents to breed and rear children. Some couples might be fit to breed but not rear and these would give up their children — or the reverse. (*The Leader*, March 11-18, 1982, p. 6)
   The Chairman of the North Carolina 2000 Commission was University of North Carolina President William C. Friday. He wrote a glowing foreword to world federalist George W. Blount's *Peace Through World Government* and also pledged when the study began in 1981 to look closely at the state's *quality of life* in the year 2000.
   Quality of life is a much-used term among the world's redistribution-of-wealth advocates. It was also the basis for Nazi Germany's elimination of non-persons and useless eaters. (The communists don't bother with a screening process. They just kill everybody).
   Dr. Elizabeth D. Koontz was the vice chair of North Carolina 2000. She was assistant state superintendent of the North Carolina Department of Public Instruction, nationally recognized leader in the Women's Movement, state chair of NC-IWY, national delegate to United Nation's Commission on Status of Women, chair for Panel on International Education K-12, former NEA President, board member on SIECUS (humanist). During the Nixon administration she pushed for an arrangement like the kibbutz houses for children which would take them, even at birth, for the state to raise.

   Governor Hunt is running against Senator Jesse Helms for the U.S. Senate seat in North Carolina.
   Let's look at Jim Hunt's connections.

In the *York Daily Record*, August 27, 1983, a small article discussed former California Governor Jerry Brown's efforts to "further his global education by meeting with Mexican manufacturing moguls, French President Francois Mitterand and German leaders in Bonn . . . Brown's Political Action Committee has begun a series of fund raisers . . . that are expected to raise over 100,000 anti-Helms dollars . . ."

Francois Mitterand had just months before nationalized all church schools in France that had accepted government assistance through tuition tax credits (*Morris Report,* March 1983, p. 1 and *The Kansas City Times,* December 22, 1982). Barbara Morris has done a careful study on this topic and it is called *Tuition Tax Credits.*

An End

All books used in public schools carry an International Standard Book Number (ISBN) which is different for each edition of each book. This allows each school system to inventory each school's supply of books and update the inventory as new purchases are made. Eventually all "obsolete" or "non-text" will be eliminated so only "approved" books (1984 Big Brother Books) will be available to school children.

If you have access to a copy of *Behavioral Science Teacher Education Program* (B Step) completed in 1969 through an HEW grant, examine it carefully. An item of special interest on page 129 is the Universal Birth Number which codes the global area, birth registration number and year of birth. There is also a personal identification number explained on pages 29 and 30.

CHAPTER 9

Why the American Dream Has Become A Nightmare

If you control youth you control the future.
If you control money you control politicians.
If you control politicians you control government
If you control government you control the youth

None of the above thoughts is original. But this order helps us understand some interesting facts. For instance, no matter which party wins in an election, nothing changes. And no matter who becomes president, nothing changes.

Christians must run for office. Government is "dirty," because godly men are not governing. Men of God can make mistakes but because they seek the wisdom in the scriptures they make fewer mistakes. When God is involved, even our mistakes can be turned to something good.

Convinced that Christians must take over the political life of the nation, I persuaded my young friend Doug, who was an assistant pastor at a local church, to file and run for a seat on the county council. Together we attended a seminar on how to run a campaign and went through the usual procedures to get him on the ballot. His family had been in the county for a long time, he had been educated in its school system, he was well known and well liked and had many contacts. The incumbent had decided to run for a seat in the Maryland General Assembly so all systems read "go." I was Doug's campaign manager even though I had lived in the county only a short time and didn't know a lot of people. But I did know how to dial a phone and solicit help.

But the Lord had other plans.

On Friday before the Fourth of July, 1980 which fell on a Sunday, Doug called and sadly announced he would be unable to run for the council seat. Since Monday was a holiday, he would have to withdraw on Tuesday. That was the last day to enter or drop out of the race.

I was convinced "I" could change his mind before the deadline. Doug, his senior pastor and a seminary student agreed to pray together and separately about Doug's candidacy. I was to meet with Doug Saturday evening.

Saturday morning Doug called and I could tell by the happy tone of his voice that he had good news for me. He was going to run!

No I was wrong. All three men, while in prayer, kept receiving one name to run — Bill Bowen.

The impossibility and absurdity of such a suggestion provoked dozens of reasons why I could never run for the office. I immediately had Penny call our pastor, Dr. John Dekker. A close personal friend, he would know how busy Penny and I were with speaking engagements on globalism and education. His own ministry, "In Defense of Truth," gave him little free time so he would surely agree that I shouldn't run.

A few hours later he telephoned his answer back and said, "Run!"

Stunned, I asked Penny to call Pastor McKnight, another friend, and seek his counsel.

Again, "Run!" That was three out of three.

"But Lord," I prayed, "practically all the campaign funds have been spent! All the bumper stickers and posters have Doug's name on them! No one knows me in Harford County! I'm going to be away on speaking engagements during the campaign! I won't make it through the primary! There isn't enough time! . . . do I have to?"

Tuesday, just hours before the filing deadline, Penny, Doug and I met at the Board of Election Supervisors. I became the candidate and Doug became the treasurer-campaign manager.

We won in the primary. Ironically the first advice I received was to "play down my Christianity bit. Just talk about landfills and other issues. You can get into the religious stuff later."

It sounded like good advice and came from veteran politicos and I wanted to win.

Then another thought came to me. It was very clear but kind. "Are you ashamed of Me?" the still small voice asked. The whole purpose of Doug or me running was to render a humble offering of service to the Lord.

When we candidates had an opportunity to speak, my opening remarks at every campaign engagement were: "I am a Christian. I believe in Christian morality. If you don't believe in such standards, DO NOT vote for me, because you will be disappointed. You won't get politics as usual if I win." I don't recommend this practice for other candidates but I wanted to make it clear to God, to myself and the people why I was a candidate.

It was a tough race. My opponent was not a principled man and he was skilled in political deceit. I resolved that my campaign would not be directed to defeating him but to winning the race. There was a peace in this approach and I knew that if I won, it was God's will and His victory. If

I lost, He had other things for me to do.

The Lord became my Campaign Manager working through Penny and Doug. Other Christians — men I didn't even know — who had been defeated in the primary took their signs down, repainted them with my name and put them up again. Churches began to rally. The Spirit of God moved.

We won — the Lord and His people. Some races with veteran candidates were lost by 60 votes. The Lord gave us a 2000-vote majority which is a sizeable margin in a county race. As returns came in members of the press were commenting so I could hear, "Can we still throw Christians to the lions?" "Can you believe it? That fundamentalist is winning!"

When asked by the reporters, "To what do you attribute your victory?" I could only make one truthful reply, "I owe it to God."

"I can't print that!" was one reporter's reaction.

"You will this time, because it's true," I replied. She reported it just that way.

I share this story in detail because my God is a here-and-now God. I weep quietly sometimes when confronted with the fact that He cared for someone as unworthy as me and helped me win.

I want to encourage fellow Christians to be on the Lord's side. It's going to be tough by the world's standards but far more rewarding than the world.

Silver and gold have I none, but such as I have, give I thee. In the name of Jesus Christ of Nazareth, rise up and walk.   Acts 3:6

Rise up. Walk. We have work to do. The Lord has a world to heal.

Stewardship

Do you have any idea how our government spends *our* money? I don't. Yet if we were to turn as much money over to an individual as we give to our government, we would very carefully check every expenditure made by the individual. The people of this country never know where their tax dollars go. I am appalled when I read of millions going to alien governments hostile to us, yet our debt each year is so vast I can't comprehend the quantities of money involved.

It is equally incomprehensible and infuriating to discover great sums of money being wasted on domestic programs of no merit or on issues completely contrary to the best interests of the general welfare, although supposedly being spent for that general welfare.

One of the quickest ways for the people to regain control of our government is to cut off the wasteful use of our nation's bounty — the financial as well as the natural resources. To do that we must control the government offices that in turn manage our nation's finances.

If all Christians were to register and vote we would control every elected office in our nation — from president to dog catcher.

So often during my campaign people would say they would vote for me but they weren't registered. These people were in their 60s. I guess there never really was a time when we could trust the government to others but it is especially true in these times.

During my campaign I visited a senior class in a Christian school. After the discussion I asked how many were eighteen years old. All but a few raised their hands. I then asked how many were registered to vote. Not one hand was raised. In my social studies classes in the public school there would have been only one or two hands not raised.

I believe we owe a debt to our God for blessing us with

such a bountiful haven; to our Founding Fathers who conquered the hardship involved in civilizing the country and created a republic based on biblical principles; to our parents who preserved the republic; and to our children who are the heirs to this great land. As believers we are required to be good stewards, yet we surrender it all to non-believers and expect them to preserve it for us.

International Bankers

International bankers are evil people. They are traitors to the nation in which they hold their citizenship. They do not see themselves in such a light. Their purpose is to create a world monopoly of all wealth. Yet they don't understand:

For what does it profit a man to gain the whole world, and forfeit his soul?
Mark 8:36

They have residences in many nations, travel freely throughout the world and have money interests that cross national boundaries. Their love of money and the power it creates deafens their ears and blinds their eyes to national loyalties which to them represent impediments to their global monetary interests.

Since they envision themselves as the rulers of the new global government that is to replace the many national governments, they see only benefits in such a merger. They understand mergers and conglomerates. To them, nationalism is petty and provincial.

Their wealth and power provides them with many ambitious outsiders — sycophants very willing to do their bidding. They buy and destroy presidents, dictators and monarchies. They dictate to the White House, the Kremlin, and Buckingham Palace (and 10 Downing Street). They manipulate congress, parliament and the politburo.

The Obsolete Dollar

The Rockefellers, Carnegies and Morgans are now the Rockefellers, Wristons and Hammers. The go-fers are the Nixons, the Kissingers, the Carters and the Bushs. Although education has been the vehicle to humanize, socialize, and communize us, the complete take over will come through an economic catastrophe. Most likely it will be the result of a bankruptcy of the United States government. That will trigger a devaluation of money and lead to a stock market crash. This will bring on a world depression — and a global government which will be thought necessary to solve all our problems.

The dominoes are in place. The more a government is in debt the easier it is for the global bankers to control it. The loans come with higher interest rates (which cause more debt) and more strings attached.

This will happen not because of the evil in them but because of the lawlessness in us.

It is our covetousness that gives these men power over us because the same biblical laws that tell us to owe no man applies to our government. Why haven't we come against this? Because we are not content with the full measure the Lord has given us. We want more for ourselves so we go into debt — to such an extent that our creditors own everything we have. Instead of living within the means provided by God we let our covetousness make us slaves to unbelievers. OUR government reflects OUR values and beliefs. If we had known the Word of God as well as we know our TV schedules we wouldn't have fallen for humanism, TM, EST and man-centered, mind-over-matter positivism nonsense.

Do not trust in princes, In mortal man, in whom there is no salvation.
                              Psalm 146:3

Well, we're in hock and so is our nation. How did it happen?

The Federal Reserve Hoax

The Jekyll Island story is not new. For those who are familiar with it or have read *Honest Money* by Dr. Charles Norburn (1983) or *None Dare Call it Conspiracy* by Gary Allen (1972) you may wish to skip this section.

Dr. Cleon Skousen of the Freemen Institute has published a monograph entitled "The Urgent Need for a Comprehensive Monetary Reform" (1982) that summarizes the Federal Reserve sections in the two books previously mentioned. All of these men have good research and agree that the Federal Reserve must be abolished if our nation is to escape a rapidly approaching financial disaster. A loose and imprudent money policy will cause any government to collapse. A dictatorship always follows.

In the fall of 1910 a secret meeting took place for nine days at the J. P. Morgan estate on Jekyll Island, Georgia. Present were Senator Nelson Aldrich (Nelson Aldrich Rockefeller was named after his maternal grandfather); A. P. Andrew (assistant secretary of the treasury); Frank A. Valderlip (president of Rockefeller's National Bank of New York City); Henry P. Dawson (senior partner of J. P. Morgan & Co.); Charles D. Norton (president of Morgan's First National Bank of New York); Benjamin Strong of Morgan's Bankers Trust Company (New York central office); and Paul Warburg (partner in Kuhn, Loeb & Co. of New York. He bought his partnershp with Rothschild money. His brother Max was later a major financier of the Russian Revolution and all the Warburgs helped finance Adolph Hitler).

Their objectives known as the Aldrich Plan was to create a centralized bank.

The Bank of England, Bank of France and the Bank of Germany are not government banks but privately owned monopolies just as the Federal Reserve. These monopolies are granted in return for loans. Once the government is in debt to the bankers, the bankers are in control. Lenin said that the establishment of a central bank was ninety percent of communizing a government. Keep in mind section five of *The Communist Manifesto.*

The Aldrich Plan ran into trouble because a House of Representatives investigation had exposed the involvement of Rockefeller and Morgan in the crash of 1907 and 1908. Also, President Taft was opposed to it. Since it couldn't be passed as a Republican measure it was renamed the Federal Reserve System and it became a democratic proposal.

The international bankers in reality involved both parties so their plan involved defeating Taft and electing Woodrow Wilson, the Democratic candidate. Wilson was much more to their liking anyway. He had been a student of Richard T. Ely, the founder and first secretary of the American Economic Association (AEA). Ely had received his Ph. D. at Heidelberg and brought back the collectivist philosophy of Hegel and applied it to economics. His first book was *French And German Socialism,* written as a member of Daniel Gilman's staff at The Hopkins. His AEA was so powerful that free enterprise economics to this day cannot be found as a departmental policy on an American university campus.

It was now necessary to stop William Howard Taft who looked like a sure winner. By flattering Teddy Roosevelt, the Wall Streeters were able to get him to run against Taft, who had been his hand-picked successor. To keep Wilson on target Edward Mandel House became Wilson's constant companion. In his book *Philip Dru: Administrator* House dreamed of establishing a social state on Marxian principles. House wanted a central bank and a graduated income tax, both provisions of *The Communist Manifesto.* Both of these measures were enacted during Wilson's presidency. Yet none of the benefits promised by these measures have been realized.

The number four item on the government's debt list is the interest paid to the Federal Reserve for RENTING the money from them that we print to run the government!

The Federal Reserve has never been audited nor called to account for its policies. It is completely beyond the Congress. It amasses huge profits from our government. This money could be used to retire our national debt and would make the federal income tax totally unnecessary. Can you imagine the bliss of being rid of the federal debt, the Federal Reserve, the federal income tax and the "Infernal" Revenue Service!

According to the *Don Bell Report,* January 14, 1983:
★ 50 percent of the Michigan farmers are in trouble.
★ 200 farmers in Springfield, Colorado, stormed the courthouse demanding that farm foreclosures be stopped.

This is an all-pervasive problem. It is the independent family farmer who is facing foreclosure because of the Federal Reserve interest policies. It is the smaller community banks that are in danger of failing or merging with the international bankers. Just read the small notices in the business section of your local newspaper. There are almost daily items on failure and mergers.

Inflation is larceny and the major cause of economic instability.

We should not try to untangle this maze created to bewilder the American citizenry. Our Congress has the power simply to cut us off from these financially destructive inflationary powers.

During the Reagan administration millions of dollars have been given to the international bankers presumably to save them from ruin because of their loans to COMMUNIST countries!

Congressman Ron Paul of Texas explained in the June 8, 1981 *The Spotlight* that:

1) the House Banking Committee gave $13 billion in taxpayers money to the World Bank. (Robert McNamara, former secretary of defense and member of the World Future society, just resigned as president of the World Bank).

2) The World Bank transferred the money to its affiliates, the International Development Association, the Latin American, Asian and African development banks.

3) The money is then borrowed by the foreign interests who give it to the American international banks to buy American investments such as acreage, mineral leases, hotels, etc.

4) The money was to render aid to the poor of the world.

In the August 1981 issue of *Readers Digest* it was noted that all the billions of dollars given to the Export-Import Bank "has benefited only a handful of huge corporations."

On February 20, 1983, the U.S. taxpayers paid $120 million on the Polish debt which is held by the international bankers who get their money to loan to these communist countries from the American tax dollars given to the World Bank and its affiliates. A short time later the same was done for communist Romania. Remember these are the governments under the economic system that was to solve all the economic problems of the world.

If you have become a co-maker in debt, deliver yourself
as quickly as possible from whomever the debt is owed.
Proverbs 6:1,5

Let's look at some interesting items about North Carolina in Dr. Charles Norburn's *Honest Money,* p. 101:

October 1982 — Kuwait holds oil and mineral leases on western North Carolina government land.

December 6, 1982 — Foreign investments in North Carolina exceed $100 billion and hold $250 billion in stocks and government bonds.

Tens of thousands of acres in rich eastern North Carolina farm land have been bought up by foreign investors:

★ 54,000 acres, Open Grounds Farm, Carteret County, Owners: Italian

★ 7,000 acres, the Shima American, Washington County, Owners: Japanese

★ 380,000 acres, the First Colony Farmers, Washington, Terrel, Hyde and Dale Counties, Owners: Malcome McLean of New Jersey in escrow for "unidentified foreign interests."

Foreign investors in Texas, Louisiana, Kansas, Mississippi and other states now approach twelve million acres.

Indebtedness enslaves our children and our lands belong to foreigners.
Nehemiah 5:5

What do our globalists say?

"An end run around national sovereignty, eroding it piece by piece, will accomplish much more than the old-fashioned frontal assault."
Richard Gardner, *Foreign Affairs,*
Vol. 52, No. 3, p. 558

"I believe . . . there exists an extraordinary opportunity to achieve for the first time a truly global society, carried by the prinicple of interdependence."
Henry Kissinger, *International Educational Cultural Exchange,* Summer 1976, p. 35.

"The 'new world order' is to be first constructed in non-

military areas."
                              Kingman Brewster, p. 140
                              Foreign Affairs, April 1972

"Scientific-international linkage . . . would encourage
an international educational system."
                              Zbigniew Brzezinski,
                              Between Two Ages, p. 299

Regionalism and Metro

Every topic covered in this book, *Globalism: America's
Demise,* has probably been the topic of one or more
books that discuss in detail the history and intent of each
topic. Our society has become so programmed against
reading that the enemy has effectively cut us off from
major sources of written information.

I encourage you, however, to read what you can get
your hands on about these topics while printed information is still available. One auditory information access is
cassette tapes but these have documentation limits.

I have found very limited printed coverage of regionalism
and Metro. Fortunately what is in print is very good. Jo
Hindman has written several — *The Metrocrats, Blame
Metro* and *Terrible 1313 Revisited.* Archibald E. Roberts,
Lt. Col. AUS Ret., has authored *Emerging Struggle for State
Sovereignty* and several other books which not only ex-
pose the globalist efforts at the regional and community
level but provide guidelines of action for the informed
Christian and American patriot.

Although the implementation of regionalism was fairly
recent, the idea was not new. It was in violation of Article
IV, Section 3 of the Constitution which reads:

". . . no new State shall be formed or erected within the
jurisdiction of any other State; nor any State be formed by
the junction of two or more States, or parts of States,

without the consent of the legislatures of the States, concerned as well as Congress."

The White House Directive, March 27, 1969, "Restructuring of Government Service Systems," created ten regions to administer the fifty states with a subcapital in each region. This was set up by President Nixon who had campaigned on a conservative republican platform. We must learn quickly that republican does not equal conservative and that conservative does not equal Christian.

"Colonel" House, the alter ego of President Wilson, had postulated that we should have two political parties. this would give the impression that the American people had a choice but only one ideology and that would be one-world socialism. (Henry Kissinger, former secretary of state, was President Nixon's "Colonel" House).

Despite Nixon's high visability as vice president in Eisenhower's administration, he was unable to win in his 1960 bid for president. He couldn't even win the governorship of California after being vice president of the United States. He later appeared in New York with an expensive office and under the wing of the Rockefellers, runs and wins the presidency.

Other than Watergate — which is a process (Reagan nearly got himself watergated — and assassinated — before he learned to "cooperate") not an event — what is pointed to in Nixon's administration as his most significant "accomplishment?" It was the recognition of Red China which eventually led to the removal of Nationalist China from the United Nations Security Council. This also legalized Dr. Armand Hammer's trade with Red China. Dr. Hammer is a super-globalist and founder of the World Colleges along with the late Count Mountbatten and now Prince Charles of England.

Global government must control the people. (Population roll back is to reduce world population to a controllable number. It is not just to get it in line with natural resources which daily are being revealed as virtually unlimited even in the light of our present population. The only surplus population we need to worry about is the government bureaucrats who oppress and drain the substance of the productive population).

The basic principle of the regional and metro systems is to concentrate power in the administrative sector at all levels from global dictator to regions to Newstates to metro centers to the neighborhood. This by-passes the states, which are mini-republics, their assemblies as well as Congress. Group *consensus* or peer pressure, which would be programmed by operant conditioning via the cradle-to-grave community school, would compel conformity. Dissidents, who would include Christians who refuse conversion to the global New Age religion (drug, alcohol and other debilitating escape mechanisms will be withdrawn. Eastern cult mechanisms such as mantras, TM and non-reproductive sex, provide euphoric escapes but the workers remain productive laborers and can care for themselves) and national patriots would be assigned to a government concentration camp.

At present there are ten such camps, one in each region and operated by the Department of Defense. The largest is in Alaska southeast of Fairbanks and is for dissidents classified as mentally ill. Don't forget that the humanists running our government and our children — which they program in the public schools — think any one who believes in God is insane.

We have to control church schools because fundamental, Bible-believing Christians do not have the right to indoctrinate their children in their faith, because we, the state, are preparing all children for the Year 2000, when America will be part of the One World Global Society and their children won't fit in.

— Stated on Channel 6 in Omaha, Nebraska by a state legislator, the head of the state PTA, and the lobbyists for the NEA and the state school board.

This kind of treatment (as received by John Hinckley — family friend of Vice President Bush — for his attempted assassination of President Reagan) is provided by the Uniform Mental Health Act and administered nationally by HEW.

President Reagan revoked the Executive Order 12314, which established the Federal Regional Councils, with his own Executive Order No. 12407 of February 22, 1983. I suspect it will put to sleep the anti-regional forces but will be ignored by the regionalists just as Secretary Bell has ignored his mandate to dismantle the Department of Education.

What concerns me greatly about the metro program — there are many issues of concern — is the consolidation of law enforcement agencies such as police and sheriff departments under regional controls and the neutralization of police efforts at law enforcement with "soft tactics." ("Soft tactics" are to law enforcement what the First Earth Battalion is to the military).

This aspect of Metro is removing the police agencies from the role of protection for the people to enforcers for the government. There's a big difference between these concepts — protector and enforcer.

The total program of the globalists and the regional plan for governance are not too different from what existed in the Dark Ages — and I suspect it will be a dark time when God is outlawed.

And this is the message we have heard from Him and announce to you, that God is light, and in Him there is no darkness at all. If we say that we have fellowship with Him and yet walk in the darkness, we lie and do not practice the

truth.
                    1 John 1:5,6

Travel will be limited. What few needs the rulers will acknowledge will be provided locally and the citizen-serfs will live and die within a small city-state or fiefdom. This idea was introduced to President Franklin Roosevelt by Dr. Jacob Moreno, who immigrated to the United States in 1925. Moreno boasted that he had come to bring his social-change philosophy to the United States rather than to Soviet Russia. He said another fellow, Karl Marx, already had established a similar system in the U.S.S.R. The "model cities" program is identical to that envisioned by Moreno — and those in Red China and Soviet Russia.

A new constitution to legalize regionalism is already written and waiting. I do not want a new constitutional convention filled with socialist heathens. The author of the new constitution was Rexford Tugwell, a member of FDR's brain-less trust and longtime propagandist for international banking interests. He was also FDR's assistant secretary of agriculture. He once predicted that the use of all land, public and private, one day will be controlled by the government. Land which cannot be operated effectively under private ownership will be held by the government.

"We have depended too long on the hope that private ownership and control would operate somehow for the benefit of society as a whole. That hope has not been realized ... We already have too many farmers," he said.

The Newstates Constitution of Tugwell was funded by the Ford Foundation at a cost of $25,000,000. Foundation funds are tax exempt which means we paid extra taxes to finance this subversion.

CHAPTER 10

Somewhere Over the Rainbow Is a Fabian Socialist World

In the new world order the globalists will put prayer and religious studies back into the public schools. These studies will at times include Christianity. There will also be teaching on a type of Judeo-Christian religiosity — among all the other teachings the children will receive. But remember the one world government will have a one world church.

Conflict — Resolution — Change

The removal of prayer from public schools by the Supreme Court decision in the Madalyn Murray case occurred with little Christian opposition. We were all busy pursuing the "good life, here and now," as if we were humanists instead of believers.

As children became more humanized and Simonized problems began to arise — and to be publicized. The removal of Bible reading and prayer from schools had created problems. As time went on the problems were being widely discussed.

Christian communities, formerly reconciled to a separation of church and state, were being prodded to make a public stand against the secularization of the nation. Congressmen and other office holders were being petitioned and lobbied to support prayer amendments and similar legislation. The ACLU and the American Jewish Committee continued their conflict — resolution — change strategy by attacking Christmas manger scenes and Easter observances on public property, stirring up more Christian reaction.

The next step will be a solution!

On October 2-4, 1983, a colloquium was held on the twentieth anniversary of the Schempp-Murray Supreme Court decisions in Indianapolis, Indiana. It was conducted by the National Council on Religion and Public Education (NCRPE). The topic was "Religion in Public Schools." The purpose was:

> To provide a forum and means for *cooperation* among organizations and institutions concerned with those ways of studying *religion* which are educationally appropriate and constitutionally acceptable to a *secular* program of public education.
> – NCRPE registration form, p. 1 (Emphasis added).

Note that Christianity is not mentioned, only religion and that the intent is secular. The conference was funded by grants from the Lilly Foundation and the Gemmer Foundation. The keynote speaker was a professor from the Harvard Divinity School, hardly the citadel of orthodox Christian theology. One of the plenary speakers was a professor emeritus from the Cornell Law School, again hardly a seat of learning for traditional, constitutional law. A third plenary speaker (there were only five) was the executive for religious and civil liberty in the NATIONAL

COUNCIL OF CHURCHES! Another plenary speaker was a superintendent of a public school system.

Of interest in the NCRPE promotional material is a quote from Chief Justice Clark's reaffirmation of his unconstitutional doctrine of neutrality in the Abington v. Schempp and Murray v. Curlett cases, "One's education is not complete without a study of *comparative religion* or the history of religion and its relation to the advancement of civilization . . ." Again, note that he refers to religion and not Christianity and "comparative religion" which is compatible with the doctrine of neutrality.

Many Christians, hoping to restore even a small portion of their beliefs to the public domain, will unwittingly allow the One True God to occupy a lesser place among the many man-centered religious cults of the East. All of the Eastern religions are based on the beliefs of a man — Buddha, Confuscius and others — striving for godship through his own efforts and works. If the cross of Calvary were the ultimate humiliation for Our Savior, this new Christian appeasement must be the next in order.

How will the One True God and His Divine Word fare in the comparative religion classes?

In 1976 (the year of the Declaration of Interdependence — a Year of Infamy) the National Council of Teachers of English — which is the English teachers' branch of the NEA — published an article, "The Bible Presented Objectively," in the January 1976 issue of *Language Arts*.

I suspect it was deliberate that this proposal was made during that year.

The article stated that the Genesis account of creation will be taught as *myth* so as not to disturb the children's "equanimity" in accepting other more "sophisticated scientific explanations of world origins."

"No creation would be 'the right one'. . . Yahweh's would be used along with the creation myths found in Norse mythology, American Indian lore, and Sumerian epic." The article said ALL of these are pagan and alien to our heritage!

Samuel I and II might be taught as Jewish history. Bible figures would be portrayed as legendary.

"Bible myths would be used with other myths," i.e., "in tandem with non-religious materials" or myths such as Aesop's Fables and African legends, according to the article. The literary and historical value of the Bible would be "appropriate to the secular function of the public schools" but "the moral teachings of the Bible" would not be acceptable. Bible heroes would be compared to such secular "heroes" as Billy Jean King, Frederick Douglas, Ulysses and Robin Hood.

The author of the article had some words of caution:
> "I would caution against the over-use of church-house publications . . . Theological bias may tend to slip in . . .

> "It is essential for the teacher to be constantly aware of the need for and value of objective presentation.

> "I would urge judicious use of New Testament materials.

> ". . . enthusiasm for a particular sectarian point of view is taboo.

> ". . . *neutral* versions of Christ's birth but . . . only in conjunction with legends of other cultures and religions so as to remove any charge of Christian *bias*. Certainly Jesus is *at least* a culture hero, and . . . here lies trouble . . . if the teacher . . . does not include figures central to *other religions* like Buddha, Mohammed, or Lao Tse."

Why must a Christian nation be ashamed of its own God and religious heritage? To accept false religions on a parity with Christ is to worship false gods!

What Has The New Age To Do With All This?

Comparative religions is the New Age answer to the belated wailing of Christians over their loss of religious supremacy in the nation God gave to them. It is part of the conflict — solution — change formula of the globalists. This is why I oppose a prayer amendment and especially silent prayer. I want to know what is being prayed and more importantly to whom. The prayer amendment doesn't provide an answer to either of these concerns. It doesn't specify — in a so-called Christian nation — to whom we are to pray. I'm not interested in guaranteeing the right of pagans to pray to Satan. So if the amendment isn't an audible Christian prayer amendment then I don't want any such amendment.

If the Supreme Court, Congress, the president and the nation can ignore the first amendment guarantee of freedom of religion, what is going to make anyone respect the prayer amendment? The only thing a silent prayer amendment will accomplish is to give Satanic pagan cults parity with Christianity and I am unalterably opposed to that.

Anyone who wants to can pray silently right now anywhere in the world, including Communist countries where prayer and other religious practices etc., are forbidden. It isn't hard to see that the covert pagan benefits of a silent prayer amendment will greatly outweigh the overt Christian benefits. Obviously not everyone supporting such an amendment is on the Lord's side.

Let me recommend that everyone who can secure a copy of Constance Cumbey's well-researched book *The Hidden Dangers of the Rainbow,* Huntington House, Inc., 1983. What is so valuable about this book is the detailed documentation of the multitude of cults that have infiltrated our society. The Christian elect need to have ready access to this information. You will discover that most of the educational buzz words such as holistic, pluralistic,

"We struggle not against flesh and blood..."

multiethnic, valuing, etc., are part of the New Age vocabulary. The same promoters of progressive, values-free education are found among the list of New Agers, Planetary Citizens and other such groups.

Once during a flight on American Airlines I noticed their magazine is called *American Way*. What a coincidence that AA would use the same name as Norman Lear's group, People for the American Way (PAW). Norman Lear is a humanist, futurist, liberal.

Besides millions of dollars, what does he have in common with an airline? In skimming through some of the articles I found one dealing with dancers in Broadway productions being made to partake in sensitivity training; another article on left brain-right brain functions, holistic thinking, etc.

I then turned to the editorial page and found — with no surpise — that Isaac Asimov, Planetary Citizen, humanist futurist and author of sci-fi books loved by children, was not only a contributing editor but the editor for "Change" in the American Airlines magazine. There is no such thing as coincidence.

What's Syncretism?

Sir Julian Huxley, atheist, fellow traveler, former director general of the anti-American UNESCO, declared that the United Nations cannot base itself on any *one* religion. The only alternative would be a synthesis of *all* religions as a spiritual foundation of the United Nations.

This concept can be summarized as:

1) All religions are one in origin and based on a common principle of brotherhood.
2) Differences are "accidental" caused by misunderstanding of the common principle.
3) All religions must merge into a Universal Brotherhood.

The idea is that any religon that insists on remaining separate must be eliminated. This would be the only way to achieve world peace.

And they have healed the brokenness of My people superficially, Saying, 'Peace, peace,' But there is no peace.
Jeremiah 6:14

Ecumenism is not the same as syncretism. Syncretism is a merger of all religions, whereas ecumenism is limited to Christians. The World Council of Churches (WCC) has redefined "ecumenical" to mean all the inhabitants of the world but the WCC doesn't even pretend to be Christian any longer. (See Bernard Smith, *Approaches* Magazine, August 1974. Also John Cotter, *A Study in Syncretism*, p. 12).

Among the advocates of syncretism, or one world religion, are the leaders in Planetary Initiative, the New Age Movement, futurism, globalism, Fabian socialism, humanism, etc.

Those advocates include Fabian George Bernard Shaw, Planetary Citizen Yehudi Menuhin, Theosophy founder Madame Blavatsky, Guardian of the Buhai Faith Abdul'l Baha, Alice Bailey and pro-communist historian and syndicated columnist Arnold Toynbee. Toynbee was a mentor of the Esalen Encounter center in California until his death in 1975.

In 1946, just one year after the United Nations was established, the World Spiritual Council, a Universal Brotherhood organization, began. This became the religious counterpart to the United Nations World Government or World Federalist Movement. Among its members were President Eisenhower, John Foster Dulles, Allen W. Dulles (former CIA chief), Henry Luce (*Time* and *Life* owner), George Meany (AFL-CIO president), Norman Thomas (socialist presidential candidate), Eleanor Roosevelt, John F. Kennedy, Chief Justice Earl Warren,

Prince Bernhard of the Netherlands (former head of the Bilderbergers) and the Shah of Iran.

The first congress of World Fellowship of Faiths (WFF) was held in 1933 in Chicago with former President Herbert Hoover and Jane Addams — a communist spinster and business partner with Nicolai Lenin in the Russian-American Industrial Corporation — presiding.

One of the nine American leaders of the Baha'i faith is Dwight W. Allen, a left-leaning ultra-radical who is head of the School of Education, University of Massachusetts. He attended the White House Conference on Children in 1970. The Bahais' program parallels closely the one world religion and one world government movements and was the first to call for a world police force and world peace movement.

They follow their program to the smallest detail. Planetary Citizens is a Bahai movement connected with UNICEF.

Minneapolis students, members of the United Nations Association of Minnesota, wrote and starred in a film, "Take a Trip on Spaceship Earth." The film encourages school children to register as planetary citizens and then conduct a planetary citizenship registration drive at their school, church or neighborhood. They receive Planetary Citizens T-shirts, pins, bumper stickers and posters as well as subscriptions to *Planet Earth* journal and *One Family* newsletter.

Isaac Asimov is a Planetary Citizen and also coordinator in New York City for the World Government of World Citizens. Yehudi Menuhin is another Planetary Citizen and world Citizen along with Linus Pauling, Corretta Scott King — widow of Martin Luther King — Princess Juliana of the Netherlands., Roy Amara, Theodore Hesburg — president of Notre Dame — Ervin Laszlo, Club of Rome and David Spangler. All are Planetary Citizens.

From June 17 to 21, 1983 the Planetary Initiative "met

in congress in Toronto, Canada for the purpose of developing a broadly based mandate for a. . . united world." (See Planetary Initiative Program, 1983).

World Citizens is another New Age group which has been in existence since 1953. Registrations (see replica in appendix) are in the hundreds of thousands and provide a world citizen registration number, world passport, world ID card and world birth certificate. On the back of the World Citizenship Application is a new Pledge of Allegiance to world government and "the total world community of all men, women, and children." (See Paula Taylor, *The Kids' Whole Future Catalogue,* Random House, 1982, pp. 48, 49).

B'Nai B'Rith is a Jewish branch of Freemasonry and one of two Jewish Universal Brotherhood groups. It is also closely linked to the International Jewish Alliance founded in 1860 by Adolph Cremieux.

The move toward a global religion has resulted in a number of inter-faith ceremonies. In 1951 the Festival of Britain took place in a non-sectarian church in London. In 1955 the Festival of All Faiths was held in the San Francisco Cow Palace to celebrate the tenth anniversary of the United Nations. John Foster Dulles was the U.S. National Council of Churches representative.

An identical service was held in Westminster Abbey despite widespread opposition and in defiance of a resolution passed by the 1966 Church of England Convocation at Canterbury. In the same year All-Faiths Services were held to celebrate the Queen of England's birthday.

In 1967 a World Council of Faiths was held at Cambridge University.

In 1969, the 21st anniversary of Mahatma Gandhi's assassination, was the excuse for a huge Inter-Faiths Service at St. Paul's Cathedral in London. The Archbishop of

Canterbury preached.

In 1971 an All Faiths Service was held in a Roman Catholic Church for the first time.

Some speakers at these conferences represent unusual views.

In the September 1967 conference a special service was preached by Canon Hugh Montefiore. The preceding July it was Montefiore who had postulated at the Oxford Church Conference that "Jesus was possibly a homo-sexual." (Cotter, p. 42) Montifiore was promoted to bishop in 1970.

Another speaker for the World Congress of Faiths (WCF) was Dr. Hugh Schonfield who authored the anti-Christian *The Passover Plot,* which received favorable review in the WCF journal, *World Faiths.*

Jesuit Father Tom Corbishley presided at the first inter-faith worship in a Roman Catholic Church. Corbishley was an avid admirer of humanist Teilhard de Chardin, New Age spiritualist and psychic who announced in 1979, "The Age of Nations is past: the task before us now. . . is to build the earth." (See Cotter, p. 36).

The 1975 All-Faiths Service for United Nations Day was attended by General Michael Harbottle. I mention his name in particular because he so well illustrates the net-working of the globalist programs. He is on the staff of the United Nations World Police Force, was former general-secretary of the World Disarmament Movement and be-longs to the Generals for Peace and Disarmament group. His mailing address is the United Nations Peace Academy, New York.

Queen Juliana of Holland, a Planetary Citizen and glo-balist, is a strong supporter of the interfaith movement. Her hunting lodge is available for such conferences. She threatens to "abdicate or break with NATO rather than sign a mobilization order." (See Cotter, p. 56).

These interfaith conferences include every imaginable religion, sect and cult. They actively involve individuals and groups of immense power and name recognition. The School of World Religion at Harvard is the major center for syncretism in America — and America is still a major world force.

Esperanto, which is to become the one world language, has a large role to play in the creation of a one world religion and is promoted vigorously by the interfaith advocates, even much more than the political globalists.

The World Council of Churches

If anyone belongs to a church with membership in the World Council of Churches (WCC), he must either leave that church or begin an unrelenting struggle to remove that church from the WCC. The WCC is strongly pro-communist and syncretist. It isn't a coincidence that the WCC was founded in Holland which fosters a friendly atmosphere toward syncretism.

John Foster Dulles was vice president of the WCC Commission on International Affairs, representative to the U.S. National Council of Churches, a member of World Brotherhood and CFR (as was his CIA brother, Allen). Dulles' son, Avery, is now an influential Jesuit priest.

John D. Rockefeller, Jr. gave a million-dollar grant to start the WCC Ecumenical Institute.

It was the WCC that gave financial aid for three years to American draft dodgers escaping into Canada. Millions of dollars have been channeled to communist terrorists.

Much of the WCC program is atheistic. After the retirement of Dr. Visser't Hooft as the head of WCC the organization became another agency of syncretism by simply re-defining ecumenism.

Spiritual United Nations

The immensity of this subject would fill volumes but much credit is due John Cotter for his thorough research into the background and emergence of the one world church movement entitled *A Study In Syncretism*. His work on the Temple of Understanding, the Spiritual United Nations, is especially revealing. It was fostered by the Ford Foundation and Eleanor Roosevelt. The organization was named by Mrs. Ellsworth Bunker whose husband was ambassador to India at the time (1960). Mrs J. Dickerman Hollister, a wealthy American socialite, claims to have conceived the idea in 1959.

The sponsors of the Temple are a who's who of the Fabians, globalists and New Agers. But there are also some surprises.

Following are a few sponsors: Albert Schweitzer; Eleanor Roosevelt; U Thant; former Defense Secretary Robert McNamara — once head of the World Bank; Pearl Buck; Carlos Romulo of the Philippines; John D. Rockefeller II; Margaret Sanger, founder of Planned Parenthood; the Shah of Iran; Norman Thomas; Brooks Harp, an assistant to former-President Kennedy; Bishop James A. Pike; Special Presidential Advisor Chester Bowles; Ambassador Douglas McArthur II; the president of IBM; the Society of Friends; the Unitarian Fellowship; the Jewish Theological Seminary; International Planned Parenthood; and many others.

By 1963 there were some 6,000 famous names on the sponsors list.

The Temple held the first World Spiritual Summit Conference in 1968 in Calcutta, India. Father Thomas Merton delivered the closing address and embraced strong pro-communist and one world policies. He was a member of the Communist Party prior to entering the priesthood. He authored the introduction to a new translation of the *Gita*, the "Bible" of the Hindus.

The third Spiritual Summit Conference was hosted by the Harvard University Divinity School. Keep in mind that this same school provided a main speaker for the 1983

NCRPE colloquium on "Religion in Public Schools."

Spiritual Summit V was held in 1975 — on the 30th anniversary of the United Nations, in the Cathedral Church of St. John the Divine. Among those present were Margaret Mead and astronaut Edgar Mitchell. A cosmic mass was presented five times during the week by the Sufi Order with a cast of 300 people. (It must have been a modern Tower of Babel).

At the grand finale of each performance the audience enthusiastically joined in a celebration dance.

The New Age and the Military

In mid-1979 the idea of a new army — the First Earth Battalion — was introduced by its creator, Lt. Col. Jim Channon, now retired. The headline of the *Leading Edge Bulletin* (vol. 1, no. 1) published by SRI, reads, "First Earth Battalion captures imagination of army officers ... Its essence is not physical but spiritual."

According to Channon, the concept has "infected" the highest ranks of the military. The primary allegiance of the First Earth Battalion is to the planet, not to the United States. (See Dedication page, *First Earth Battalion Manual*). The bulletin states that the soft tactics manual was an outgrowth of Channon's participation in Task Force Delta, a unit of army specialists created in 1978.

I discovered that the manual is in use by Officers Candidate Schools (OCS) and the War College in Pennsylvania. The copy I have — although a duplicate of the one used in OCS — does not carry any form or manual coding or numbering required by military documents. However, these groups are able to bypass such regulations when they deem it necessary.

Col. Channon put together a multimedia presentation about the First Earth Battalion which was shown to the senior class of the United States Military Academy at

West Point. The West Point commandant received a First Earth Battalion T-shirt. The Army financed the production of the multimedia program. The New Age Frontier of the West Coast of the United States collaborated with Channon to create the manual.

"Prepare yourself so you will be ready ... Begin your work locally until the call goes out for global action," the manual instructs (See *Manual,* p. 2). The manual is to provide the technology "to create *whole* human beings ... guidelines for the *evolution* of planetary citizen." (*Manual,* p.33)

The Battalion is to be made up of warrior monks who "envision an international ideal of service..." It calls for cooperation between the Soviets and American military. The first section or chapter of the manual is entitled "Changing Values." *The Aquarian Conspiracy* by Marilyn Ferguson is frequently cited as a resource.

In the bibliography section the writing of Teilhard de Chardin and other New Agers are the only resources listed.

The warrior monks are to evolve into gods by TM and other practices of Eastern cults and "lead the world to paradise." (See *Manual,* p. 15). The Illuminati symbol on the one dollar bill is an object lesson in symbolism for the warrior monks, who are "thinkers in the Third Wave."

The manual is like a teacher's how-to book for public education: group discussion, magic circles, consensus, transformation, actualization, networking, global consciousness, MBO, belief systems, self realization, evolving values and so forth. The army of light will conquer the enemy by blending with the enemy, becoming as one and thus resolving conflict.

Don't dismiss this as too ridiculous for the Army of the United States. In the January 23, 1984, *Time* Magazine p. 17, there is an interesting article, "An ESP Gap," on psychic weapons.

Reporter Ronald McRae has written a book, *Mind Wars,*

on the operations between the Pentagon and the psychic community. McRae claims the Defense Department has spent over $6 million in recent years on ESP, mental telepathy and parapsychology, which the military classifies as "Novel Biological Information Transfer Systems."

Physicist Russell Targ, while working at SRI International, did psychic research funded by the Defense Department or CIA. Targ is co-authoring a book called *The Mind Race.*

If you have a child in the gifted and talented school program then ESP isn't new to you or your child. In *Gifted Children Newletter,* April 1983, vol. 4, no. 4, an article entitled "Testing and Enhancing a Gifted Child's ESP" discusses how "gifted children "accept unquestioningly the telepathic and psychokinetic powers of a 'Matthew Starr' or 'ET. . .' (and) view psychic powers as logical extensions of human potential." (Sci-Fi films such as ET and Star Wars, which have biblical themes, should be critiqued carefully by Christians. These films are not teaching a doctrinal belief in Jesus Christ but in some ill defined "force").

The article encourages the use of "hypnosis and hexes as interesting tangents worth exploring." Information about the "left" and "right" brain being introduced during debriefing sessions is suggested. (Gifted and Talented programs will create a humanist elite to provide middle and upper management for the new one world order).

Bill Thomas of the *Sunpapers* staff has done an article on Jeane Dixon which included her remarks about her access to President Reagan, their friendship and her psychic advise to him.

A brief item entitled "Psychic Studies" appeared in the January 1, 1984 *Sunpapers.* It appears Prince Charles, who is chancellor of the University of Wales, would like the university to apply for funds from the Koestler Foundation to endow a professorship in parapsychology to investigate ESP, telekineses and similar subjects. (Writer Arthur Koestler and his wife committed suicide last year, 1983).

The Nebraska Scenario — A National Disgrace

Anyone who mistakenly believes that the Christian Church is not under attack by government should examine the Nebraska captivity of Dr. Everett Sileven of Louisville who refused to accept state licensure of his Christian school. The first amendment to the United States Constitution was violated when he was imprisoned and the violations ignored. The Nebraska State Constitution also was brushed aside.

We learn from the events in Nebraska that government can control any function if it has the power to license that function. The power *to grant a license implies the power* to withhold a license. Licensing carries with it the imposition of qualifications and other conditions which can be made impossible to meet. The church and church schools cannot submit to this form of control. Once such an inroad is made, the sovereignty of God becomes subordinate to Caesar.

Orwell's *1984* is here.

Our Christian beliefs have been compromised to the point that we have eyes but do not see, ears but do not hear. We Christians were oblivious to the poison which the humanists, globalists and New Agers fed us — small doses at a time — and now our tolerance has increased. Unfortunately tolerance has changed to dependence. The improprieties that shocked us a decade ago now are acceptable in this new age. We allowed this to happen because we were ignorant of the beliefs of the shapers of our times. We were also ignorant of our own Christian beliefs.

Penny, Steve and I have traveled thousands of miles together and made dozens of presentations on globalism. God's provision has made it possible for us to alert the elect concerning these dangers.

I thought I had become rather hardened to the works of the enemy. But the reality of my lectures on globalism has been brought home to me time after time. Perhaps it was the night I received a telephone call from a pastor — or his daughter – fugitives FOR justice because of their religious convictions. As they spoke I was concerned about them telling me where they were because *our phone might be tapped.*

Their crime — nothing!

Pastor Sileven's church had established a Christian school as an outreach to provide God - centered education for their children. His daughter was a successful teacher in the school and the students in the school performed well above the state and national academic scores. But because the church would not submit to Caesar and become a state-licensed school, Pastor Sileven was arrested in his pulpit and jailed. Visiting pastors were dragged from the church. The church doors were padlocked.

Even the fathers of the school children were jailed, they were arrested before Thanksgiving of 1983 and are still in jail as of this writing in 1984.

The mothers of the school children were forced to flee the state and go into hiding to escape arrest. The children were sent out of state to safeguard them from being taken from their families and made wards of the state.

Imagine the trauma experienced by these children and their families. It is not unlike the Jews being hunted and persecuted in Nazi Germany. Has a Christian holocaust begun?

Following is a ballad I heard in a Christian coffee house operated by young Christian adults as an outreach to American youth. The composer, Gary Browning, gave me permission to reproduce the lyrics.

They chained the church doors up in Louisville
They threw seven children's fathers into jail
The judge says he doesn't have to abide by the consti-
tution
He says he can do just like he feels

Refrain: The lady of justice cries out
Her hands have been bound
Judge Reagan has stolen her golden scales
The lady of justice cries out
Free the Nebraska seven
America's bleeding at the soul.

Mama, get your children out of Nebraska
In Northern Iowa there is refuge
The authorities are looking to throw you into jail and take
Your children away from you

Refrain: The lady of justice cries out
Her hands have been bound
Judge Reagan has stolen her golden scales
The lady of justice cries out
Free the Nebraska seven
America's bleeding at the soul.

Gather round, ring the bells of freedom
Tell America, tell her loud, tell her clear
Justice has been breached in Louisville, Nebraska
We must be free or destined to live in fear

Refrain: The lady of justice cries out
Her hands have been bound
Judge Reagan has stolen her golden scales
The lady of justice cries out
Free the Nebraska seven

America's bleeding at the soul.

Lyrics and music by Gary Browning, Copyright © 1984

CHAPTER 11

What To Do:
Preaching and Practicing

*But prove yourselves doers of the word, and not
merely hearers who delude themselves.*
James 1:22

Getting Prepared Spiritually

There is much we can do.

It isn't enough for you to believe in God — most unsaved people believe — we must BELIEVE GOD.

God said that He gave us (His people) dominion over
all the earth and all that is in it. Yet we hide in the shadows
of the subculture we have made for ourselves and our
families — trying to be unobtrusive.

Our children grow up convinced that being a Christian
means running away from controversy and pretending
that ungodliness does not exist. They are fearful of any
position that would lead to confrontation with the enemy.
Moody Monthly magazine (September 1982) featured

articles on the question: to where do the Christian children disappear?

The answer is that they disappear into the world. They get tired of being portrayed as "odd balls" who never have any fun and don't want anyone else to enjoy themselves. They get tired of living in a shadowy twilight zone. They don't want to hurt their parents or oppose them. So they become split personalities. They live one way at school and in the world so they can "survive" — survival is what the schools are teaching them — and follow another lifestyle when at home on weekends or in the evening with their parents, which they avoid as much as possible. They also escape into rebellion and flight.

As Christian parents and teachers we need to assert the Lordship of Jesus Christ over all His possessions — including the children. We need to do it with confidence and boldness. He promised He would provide for us and He will. God is no liar. Don't just believe in Him. Believe Him!

We need to get rid of the rapture fever. The time of our Lord's return is His business. We can't make it happen. He may tarry for years to give us time to do His work. But this work will not be accomplished if we mistakenly believe that "to occupy" merely means to occupy a pew. Unless we take a stand against ungodly rulers we will be forced to live under their tyranny.

When the righteous rule, the people rejoice,
But when a wicked man rules, people groan.
Proverbs 29:2

If we who are His people continue to ignore His work He may allow us to come under the oppression of the ungodly globalists. He has allowed this kind of oppression of His people in the past to sift them. I believe this oppression is more imminent than the rapture.

Personally I would prefer the rapture to the sifting, but His ways are not our ways.

We must also stop blaming the unsaved for what's happening in the world. The initiative is in our hands. It is our fault — the fault of the Christians — that things are as they are. We have been asleep, just as the apostles in the garden of Gethsemane when the Lord asked them to watch as He went to pray.

If My people who are called by My name humble themselves and pray, and seek My face and turn from their wicked ways, then I will hear from heaven, will forgive their sin, and will heal their land.
II Chronicles 7:14

There is more to the above scripture but most believers fail to read on.

Some of my Christian friends tell me this biblical teaching only applied to the Jews of Solomon's day. I believe it refers to all His people all the time, and I am one of His people.

But if you turn away and forsake My statutes and My commandments which I have set before you and shall go and serve other gods and worship them, then I will uproot you from my land which I have given you, and this house which I have consecrated for My name I will cast out of my sight, and I will make it a proverb and a byword among all peoples.
II Chronicles 7:19,20

He didn't rapture them out of their troubles but He did uproot them and put them through some heavy testing.

Christians are lawless. Most of us don't understand the statutes and commandments of God. We pick and choose those we do and do not want to obey. A just God won't let us get away with that.

I am constantly amazed by my own waywardness and I suspect you are, too.

Just consider our willingness to get into debt. We criticize those responsible for the national debt but are we personally following God's rules concerning stewardship?

Humanism is so compatible with our sin nature that it becomes our lifestyle without any effort on our part. It is only as I read and study the truth — *The Bible* — that I discern the counterfeit morality of the phony ideals I choose to embrace.

> *"Behold, days are coming," declares the Lord God, "When I will send a famine on the land, Not a famine for bread or a thirst for water, But rather for hearing the words of the Lord. And the people will stagger from sea to sea, And from the north even to the east; They will go to and fro to seek the word of the Lord, But they will not find it."*
> Amos 8:11,12

We Christians are to believe God's promise to provide for all our needs.

We are to occupy until He comes and not just idly wait around.

We are responsible – not the unsaved — for having allowed ungodliness to prevail in this land.

We are to know and obey all of God's word.

Getting Prepared In Other Ways

First, you should get you children out of the public schools. Our children are the only possessions we may be able to take out of this world.

> *Train up a child in the way he should go, And when he is old he will not depart from it.*
> Proverbs 22:6

The education of your children is *your* responsibility and not that of the state. If you surrender that responsibility to the state, you are still accountable before God for what your child is taught and learns.

It may be difficult to take your children out of the public schools. It may require giving up a second car or a less-affluent lifestyle in order to pay for their private-school education. But it pays eternal dividends.

When my wife Penny first placed our sons Jason and Steve in a Christian school, I really struggled to come up with their tuition. Some of our bills had to be deferred and others only partially paid during that first month. Then I was confronted with the next month's tuition.

Then the Lord began to provide. Now we pay the tuition without the many headaches we once had. The boys are worth the sacrifice and so is the Christian education they get. Parents need to be very firm about what they want their children taught and what they will not allow their children to be taught.

Second, get your church to start its own school — *tuition free* to members' children. There should be no distinction among the body of Christ as to who can and cannot afford a Christian education. The church can and should pay for it. Since your new school will not have access to taxpayers' pocketbooks, don't expect to duplicate the elegance of the public schools. Make do with what you have and go from there.

The church we now attend started its school with only three children.

Don't seek state accreditation or teacher certification. If the state comes against you it's going to be over the issue of control — not quality. Consider the Nebraska case which is only one example. There are numerous other cases still unpublicized by the "controlled" news media.

Third, get into the public schools and examine their textbooks and programs. Remember that most teachers aren't aware that they are being used as instruments to pave the way for globalism. To attack them will cause them only to defend themselves. Their human nature will dictate such a reaction. They have been so conditioned to take the blame for the failure of the public school system's academic standing and will interpret your criticism as another indictment against their professional credibility.

There are too many incompetent teachers in the classroom, but most teachers really want to do a good job. The educationists and educrats, i.e., the policy makers, have usurped all of the teachers' control over the classroom — down to each minute detail.

When I stress local control of education I refer to local government control. But the classroom teacher also needs to be put back in charge of curricula and discipline. When teachers prepared their own materials for use in the classroom, they held themselves responsible for student achievement, and the kids did very well on tests. When this practice disappeared, students' performance declined.

It is interesting that in every other profession — even the military — if a costly program fails, as miserably as education has, the general, chairman of the board or chief executive would be fired. In education the teacher is blamed for these failures, yet the teacher has no control over any policy or decision. This is why so many "good" teachers, not all, leave the profession. Higher salaries are not the answer. If pay increases could solve problems, the problems would have been solved.

We spend more on public education today than at any time in our history. Yet academic achievement is collapsing. The educrats aren't being fired because they are accomplishing exactly what they are being paid to do — reduce each successive generation to be more obedient servants of the state than the ones that came before.

It's your children to whom this is being done and your

money they are using to do it. It's time for us to do something about it.

Fourth, Christian teachers and administrators in the public schools should stay there — if they can stand it. They may be the only witness these children will ever encounter. Spend time together each day to seek the Lord. This fellowship and prayer will provide strength for teachers to stand firm in the midst of a difficult situation.

Fifth, get men involved — regardless of how difficult or inconvenient it may be. Men are the spiritual heads of the households. Women may be better educated and more articulate but God will use men in powerful ways. For too long the wives and mothers have been allowed to go to the front to do battle against the enemies of our school children. But it makes a great difference when men begin to speak out on the serious issues confronting our schools.

The more men will become involved in correcting our educational system, the faster the job will get done.

Sixth, become informed. Suggested materials are usually available through HERO or this publisher, Huntington House, Inc. Thoroughly acquaint yourself with the following:

1. Humanism

1) Review the *Humanist Manifestos* but don't buy the Prometheus edition. It is a humanist press. Don't let them grow on your money.

2) Read *Weep for Your Children,* by Dr. Murray Norris. It is a small booklet, easy to read and filled with information.

3) Read *Change Agents in the Schools* by Barbara

Morris. It is easy to read and can be used a section at a time. It is not available in commercial book stores and is more expensive — because it is self-published — but well worth the money. HERO can get them for you.

4) Have access to a copy of the *SIECUS CIRCLE*. Use this primarily as a reference book for looking up the bad guys and their organizations. Perhaps your church library or Bible group could get one to share. It is also available through HERO.

5) Keep a sense of humor. Fear immobilizes you. The Lord will have the victory.

6) Talk to school children (your neighbor's) to keep informed about what's happening. They are an endless source of information. Be specific when questioning them — but not condemning. Don't ask, "Have you studied death ed?" Instead, ask if they have visited a grave yard or written an obituary.

7) Visit the public schools. You are paying the bills for them. Become a volunteer — if you have the time. Let them be aware that you are watching and care about the schools.

8) When there are PTA meetings and other school activities ask questions and voice your concerns. School officials will try to neutralize you with the patronizing "I'm OK; You're OK" ploy. They are not programmed for any rejection so your suitable, unemotional reply — although you may want to soften it — might be, "I'm OK, because I know the Lord, but you're a jerk, if you believe in anything else." You probably can be a little more kind and still diffuse their efforts at neutralizing you. Speak your mind.

Don't be intimidated. Be firm but keep control of yourself.

2. Globalism — Remember that its basis is humanism.

1) Work to cut off the funding for any school pushing globalism.

2) Demand political accountability. Come to know your elected representatives personally. Make appointments to meet them and express some of your concerns about specific issues. Don't hit them with everything at once. Ask them to explain why they voted as they did on issues of concern to you, issues such as funding the United Nations, IMF and World Bank on the national level, humanities grants and anti-American programs at state universities and the financing of global awareness councils by community colleges on the local level. Work to get school budgets cut.

3) When your time allows, attend school board meetings. After you become familiar with the format you will feel more comfortable about addressing such bodies.

4) Write letters to public officials and forward copies to others. Send your letters to the newspaper editors, to your elected representatives and to your school board members.

5) Press the government officials for less government regulation and more tax rollbacks. Times are hard and people need this tax money that's being siphoned off by the government to fund bad programs.

3. Miscellaneous

1) Press your congressmen to have Secretary Terrell Bell write the regulations for the Hatch Amendment. This legislation was drafted to protect students' privacy from the educrats and passed unanimously by Congress in 1979!

2) Never go on an interview or appointment with "the enemy" alone. Always take a witness with you.

3) Monitor the Girl Scouts and Boy Scouts programs. These will become more controversial in the future.

4) Keep aware of the films being shown in the schools. Especially look out for *The Lottery, Future Shock* and *About Sex.* (There are two versions).

5) Teach your children that God intends for them to be Christian leaders regardless of what occupation they may choose. Encourage your Christian school to do the same.

"Whatever you do, do your work heartily, as for the Lord rather than for men." .
Colossians 3:23

6) Be the head of your home. Your children are immature and need important decisions made for them by parents who are their spiritual leaders. Don't allow rock and roll music or *Dungeons and Dragons* in your home or school. We need to be more informed about these pastimes and literature is available.

7) Start a telephone tree so the need for action and news information can be transmitted quickly. Things are that bad.

8) Don't let your children be fingerprinted.

9) Do not compromise. You are the only one who will give up anything — and the "enemy" gains.

10) Organize Nehemiah groups to become well versed in God's Word and learn to detect the efforts of the enemy. Then have the groups go to other churches and Christian assemblies to warn them of the dangers.

11) Get into politics. If politics are dirty, it's because Christians aren't involved. How can we obey Psalm 1 when we daily submit to the counsel of the ungodly? In a constitutional republic the highest office is citizen. Office holders are ordinary people just as you are but devoid of your godly wisdom. The wicked are in authority because the righteous are too busy *not getting involved.*

12) Support Christian candidates. Remember that just because a candidate is a republican it doesn't guarantee he's a Christian. If a candidate does not publicly admit his relationship to the Lord, he is ashamed of Him. How will that man later have the fortitude to stand for the Lord and resist the "go along to get along" pressures of public office?

13) Avoid litigation. It is costly and humanist judges usually rule against us. It is better for us to legislate — push for *our* laws to be passed.

14) Have voter registrations in your church and among the 18 year olds in the Christian schools.

15) Educate pastors on basic issues.

16) Get your friends and neighbors into church.

17) Plan your actions to produce positive results, e.g., get zoning and display laws against pornography, rather than just getting arrested for illegally picketing the porno shops.

18) Run for office! Even if you don't win the first time, your presence on the ballot will be taken into account by the party and the winner. It will make them more cautious in the future. Organize seminars on how to conduct a campaign. HERO has done this and it doesn't take but an hour to brief a small group of candidates on effective campaigning.

19) Make sure there are no laws or zoning codes on the books which could prohibit your holding Bible studies in your homes.

For God has not given us a spirit of fear, but of power and love and sound judgement.
2 Timothy 1:7

Has the Salt Lost It's Savor?

Christianity can make a great impact on modern America. If it turned Rome around, it can heal America.

Most people believe that our Savior was an exceptional man who lived 2000 years ago and is expected to return some time in the future. We need to let America and the world know that an unbiblical savior like that doesn't do anyone much good here and now.

My Savior is with me right now, and walks with me every day. The whole world needs that kind of relationship with Him. But that will never happen unless we share the "good news" with them.

The globalists have created a great opportunity for us to evangelize the world. We have the answer to globalism but many of us still hide in the shadows. Many of us still project an image of defeat rather than a victorious Christ and the power of the Holy Spirit.

Our lives may be the only Bible the unsaved will ever read — not in words but in works. Works will save no one, but faith without works is dead.

This godless, secular world is crumbling. People are apathetic and despairing. Our nation has lost its future. A terrible void exists. The globalists are filling this void — that they created — with a new religion of humanism. Christians should move into this void and fearlessly conquer these spiritual and physical realms.

It's time for Christians to advance! There is a lot of work to be done and there can be no compromises, no concessions and no excuses. We must walk our talk. What a glorious opportunity the enemy has created for us to witness about our Lord and Savior.

Therefore, to one who knows the right thing to do, and does not do it, to him it is sin.
James 4:17

APPENDIX A

Freemen Digest, May, 1978

A Declaration Of INTERdependence

WHEN IN THE COURSE OF HISTORY the threat of extinction confronts mankind, it is necessary for the people of The United States to declare their interdependence with the people of all nations and to embrace those principles and build those institutions which will enable mankind to survive and civilization to flourish.

Two centuries ago our forefathers brought forth a new nation; now we must join with others to bring forth a new world order. On this historic occasion it is proper that the American people should reaffirm those principles on which the United States of America was founded, acknowledge the new crises which confront them, accept the new obligations which history imposes upon them, and set forth the causes which impel them to affirm before all peoples their commitment to a Declaration of Interdependence.

We hold these truths to be self-evident: that all men are created equal; that the inequalities and injustices which afflict so much of the human race are the product of history and society, not of God or nature; that people everywhere are entitled to the blessings of life and liberty, peace and security and the realization of their full potential; that they have an inescapable moral obligation to preserve those rights for posterity; and that to achieve these ends all the peoples and nations of the globe should acknowledge their interdependence and join together to dedicate their minds and their hearts to the solution of those problems which threaten their survival.

To establish a new world order of compassion, peace, justice and security, it is essential that mankind free itself from the limitations of national prejudice, and acknowledge that the forces that unite it are incomparably deeper than those that divide it — that all people are part of one global community, dependent on one body of resources, bound together by the ties of a common humanity and associated in a common adventure on the planet Earth.

Let us then join together to vindicate and realize this great truth that mankind is one, and as one will nobly save or irreparably lose the heritage of thousands of years of civilization. And let us set forth the principles which should animate and inspire us if our civilization is to survive.

WE AFFIRM that the resources of the globe are finite, not infinite, that they are the heritage of no one nation or generation, but of all peoples, nations and of posterity, and that our deepest obligation is to transmit to that posterity a planet richer in material bounty, in beauty and in delight than we found it. Narrow notions of national sovereignty must not be permitted to curtail that obligation.

WE AFFIRM that the exploitation of the poor by the rich, and the weak by the strong violates our common humanity and denies to large segments of society the blessings of life, liberty and happiness. We recognize a moral obligation to strive for a more prudent and more equitable sharing of the resources of the earth in order to ameliorate poverty, hunger and disease.

WE AFFIRM that the resources of nature are sufficient to nourish and sustain all the present inhabitants of the globe and that there is an obligation on every society to distribute those resources equitably, along with a corollary obligation *(over)*

38

Freemen Digest, May, 1978

(Declaration cont.)

upon every society to assure that its population does not place upon Nature a burden heavier than it can bear.

WE AFFIRM our responsibility to help create conditions which will make for peace and security and to build more effective machinery for keeping peace among the nations. Because the insensate accumulation of nuclear, chemical and biological weapons threatens the survival of Mankind we call for the immediate reduction and eventual elimination of these weapons under international supervision. We deplore the reliance on force to settle disputes between nation states and between rival groups within such states.

WE AFFIRM that the oceans are the common property of mankind whose dependence on their incomparable resources of nourishment and strength will, in the next century, become crucial for human survival, and that their exploitation should be so regulated as to serve the interests of the entire globe, and of future generations.

WE AFFIRM that pollution flows with the waters and flies with the winds, that it recognizes no boundary lines and penetrates all defenses, that it works irreparable damage alike to Nature and to Mankind — threatening with extinction the life of the seas, the flora and fauna of the earth, the health of the people in cities and the countryside alike — and that it can be adequately controlled only through international cooperation.

WE AFFIRM that the exploration and utilization of outer space is a matter equally important to all the nations of the globe and that no nation can be permitted to exploit or develop the potentialities of the planetary system exclusively for its own benefit.

WE AFFIRM that the economy of all nations is a seamless web, and that no one nation can any longer effectively maintain its processes of production and monetary systems without recognizing the necessity for collaborative regulation by international authorities.

WE AFFIRM that in a civilized society, the institutions of science and the arts are never at war and call upon all nations to exempt these institutions from the claims of chauvinistic nationalism and to foster that great community of learning and creativity whose benign function it is to advance civilization and the health and happiness of mankind.

WE AFFIRM that a world without law is a world without order, and we call upon all nations to strengthen and to sustain the United Nations and its specialized agencies, and other institutions of world order, and to broaden the jurisdiction of the World Court, that these may preside over a reign of law that will not only end wars but end as well that mindless violence which terrorizes our society even in times of peace.

WE can no longer afford to make little plans, allow ourselves to be the captives of events and forces over which we have no control, consult our fears rather than our hopes. We call upon the American people, on the threshold of the third century of their national existence, to display once again that boldness, enterprise, magnanimity and vision which enabled the founders of our Republic to bring forth a new nation and inaugurate a new era in human history. The fate of humanity hangs in the balance. Throughout the globe, hearts and hopes wait upon us. We summon all Mankind to unite to meet the great challenge.

— Henry Steele Commager
October 24, 1975

Freemen Digest, May, 1978

Judiciary Sub-Committee on Impeachment-Recall

⟿ Questions and Issues ⟿

1. Does the endorsement and support of the Declaration of Inter-Dependence by a Congressman constitute the private act of an individual or is it the public act of a member of Congress?

2. Have the Congressmen who endorsed Inter-Dependence the authority to bind their office to support its international commitments?

3. Is a Congressman's legislative power circumscribed by his oath of office and the Constitution or is his authority plenary with regard to his official acts?

4. Is the endorsement and support of Inter-dependence by a Congressman, as a representative, a violation of his oath of office? In what particular?

5. Does the U.S. Attorney General have the constitutional authority to prosecute a Congressman for violating his oath of office? Has it ever been done?

6. Do the federal courts have jurisdiction to hear a controversy on what is a violation of a Congressman's oath of office or is this a political question?

7. Is Congress the exclusive tribunal for conducting the discipline of its members who violate their oath of office or is this power (also) reserved to the people and the several states under the Constitution?

Senators and Representatives who endorsed the Declaration of Interdependence:

SENATORS

James Abouresk (D-S.D.)
Edward W. Brooke (R-Mass.)
Dick Clark (D-Iowa)
Alan Cranston (D-Ca.)
Frank Church (D-Idaho)
Jacob K. Javits (R-N.Y.)
Mike Gravel (D-Alaska)
Mark Hatfield (R-Oregon)
Hubert H. Humphrey (D-Minn.)
Daniel K. Inouye (D-Hawaii)
Spark M. Matsunaga (D-Hawaii)
George McGovern (D-S.D.)
Thomas J. McIntyre (D-N.H.)
Charles McMathias (R-Maryland)
Lee Metcalf (D-Montana)
Gaylord Nelson (D-Wisconsin)
Robert Packwood (R-Oregon)
James B. Pearson (R-Kansas)
Claiborne Pell (D-R.I.)
William Proxmire (D-Wisconsin)
Abraham A. Ribicoff (D.-Connecticut)
John Sparkman (D-Alabama)
Adlai E. Stevenson, III (D-Ill.)
Harrison A. Williams, Jr. (D-N.J.)

REPRESENTATIVES

John B. Anderson (R-Illinois)
Les Aspin (D-Wisconsin)
Herman Badillo (D-N.Y.)
Max S. Baucus (D-Montana)
Berkley Bedell (D-Iowa)
Jonathan B. Bingham (D-N.Y.)

REPRESENTATIVES (continued)

Edward P. Boland, Jr. (D-Mass.)
Richard Bolling (D-Missouri)
John Brademas (D-Indiana)
George E. Brown, Jr. (D-Calif.)
William M. Brodhead (D-Michigan)
Yvonne B. Burke (D-California)
Robert Carr (D-Michigan)
Cardiss Collins (D-Illinois)
Barber L. Conable (R-N.Y.)
Silvio O. Conte (R-Massachusetts)
John J. Conyers, Jr. (D-Michigan)
James C. Corman (D-California)
George E. Danielson (D-California)
Ronald V. Dellums (D-California)
Christopher John Dodd (D-Connecticut)
Robert F. Drinan (D-Mass.)
Robert B. Duncan (D-Oregon)
Robert W. Edgar (D-Pennsylvania)
Don Edwards (D-California)
Joshua Eilberg (D-Pennsylvania)
Millicent H. Fenwick (R-N.J.)
James J. Florio (D-N.J.)
William D. Ford (D-Michigan)
Edwin B. Forsythe (R.-N.J.)
Donald M. Fraser (D-Minnesota)
Sam M. Gibbons (D-Florida)
Thomas R. Harkin (D-Iowa)
Michael Harrington (D-Mass.)
Augustus F. Hawkins (D-California)
Elizabeth Holtzman (D-N.Y.)
Frank Horton (R-N.Y.)
Barbara Jordon (D-Texas)

(cont. next page)

Freemen Digest, May, 1978

REPRESENTATIVES (cont.)

Robert W. Katsenmeir (D-Wisconsin)
Martha E. Keys (D-Kansas)
Edward I. Koch (D-N.Y.)
John J. LaFalce (D-N.Y.)
Robert R. Leggett (D-California)
Norman F. Lent (R-N.Y.)
Clarence D. Long (D-Maryland)
Paul N. McCloskey, Jr. (R-California)
Matthew F. McHugh (D-N.Y.)
Lloyd Meeds (D-Washington)
Ralph H. Metcalf (D-Illinois)
Helen D. Meyner (D-N.J.)
Abner J. Mikva (D-Illinois)
Norman Y. Mineta (D-California)
Parren J. Mitchell (D-Maryland)
John J. Moakly (D-Mass.)
William S. Moorhead (D-Penn.)
John E. Moss (D-California)
Robert N.C. Nix (D-Pennsylvania)
Richard Nolan (D-Minnesota)
Richard L. Ottinger (D-N.Y.)
Edward W. Pattison (D-N.Y.)

Claude D. Pepper (D-Florida)
Charles B. Rangel (D-N.Y.)
Henry S. Reuss (D-Wisconsin)
Frederick W. Richmond (D-N.Y.)
Peter W. Rodino, Jr. (D-N.J.)
Fred B. Rooney (D-Pennsylvania)
Benjamin Rosenthal (D-N.Y.)
Edward R. Roybal (D-California)
Leo J. Ryan (D-California)
Fernand J. St. Germain (D-R.I.)
Patricia Schroeder (D-Colorado)
John F. Seiberling, Jr. (D-Ohio)
Paul Simon (D-Illinois)
Stephen J. Solarz (D-N.Y.)
Fortney H. Stark (D-California)
Louis Stokes (D-Ohio)
Frank Thompson, Jr. (D-N.J.)
Paul E. Tsongas (D-Mass.)
Morris K. Udall (D-Arizona)
Lionel van Deerlin (D-California)

APPENDIX B

NATIONAL COUNCIL OF JUVENILE AND FAMILY COURT JUDGES

UNIVERSITY OF NEVADA
P.O. BOX 8978 • RENO, NEV. 89507

ORGANIZED MAY 22, 1937

REPRINTED FROM JUVENILE JUSTICE VOL. 27 No. 4, NOVEMBER, 1976
NATIONAL COUNCIL OF JUVENILE COURT JUDGES
BOX 8000, UNIVERSITY OF NEVADA RENO, NEVADA 89507

Model Statute for Termination
of Parental Rights

By James H. Lincoln

Introduction

In 1975, the Edna McConnell Clark Foundation funded a grant for the purpose of drafting a model statute for termination of parental rights. The Neglected Children Committee of the National Council of Juvenile Court Judges was directed to carry out this important project.

There have been a number of changes in committee membership since we undertook this project and several recently appointed members have not been involved throughout the project. The finished project represents the dedicated work of the members of the Neglected Children Committee listed below:

Hon. James H. Lincoln, Michigan, Chairman
Hon. James Delaney, Colorado
Mr. Peter Forsythe, New York
Hon. William R. Goldberg, Rhode Island
Hon. Jean Lewis, Oregon
Hon. John McGury, Illinois
Hon. David J. Thompson, Jr. (1975), Kentucky
Hon. William S. White (1975), Illinois

Ex-Officio Members:
Hon. Walter G. Whitlatch, Ohio
Hon. Margaret C. Driscoll, Connecticut
Hon. Edward V. Healey, Jr., Rhode Island
Hon. James W. Byers, Wisconsin

New Committee Members:
Hon. Frederica Brenneman, Connecticut
Hon. Richard P. Byrne, California
Hon. Ray Friederich, North Dakota
Hon. Helen Kannady, Oklahoma

Staff:
Dean Louis W. McHardy
Mr. Hunter Hurst
Ms. Marie Mildon

We are proud to present a model statute that represents the cumulative wisdom of more than a century of collective judicial experience of the members of this committee. The members have not been isolated from nor unmindful of the cross currents of the behavioral sciences which have preoccupied this nation in recent years. However, the committee has been able to test these

Author's address:
Hon. James H. Lincoln
Wayne County Juvenile Court
1025 East Forest Avenue
Detroit, Michigan 48207

JAMES H. LINCOLN

theoretical fermentations against the realities of their day-to-day practice. The proposed act is the essence of this day-to-day testing. It is simple, direct and to the point.

There is a great variety of case law and statutes relating to termination of parental rights in the fifty states. However, the merits of this proposed act have already been recognized, and even before the act assumed final form, portions of the proposed act were incorporated in legislation under consideration in both Oregon and Michigan.

The problem of setting down guidelines for termination of parental rights is as complex as human nature itself. These matters will be debated and argued to the end of time. Anyone who attempts to present a model termination statute as the last word on the matter is totally uninformed as to the complexity and difficulty of the problem. Nevertheless, we must begin an attempt at some uniformity in this maze of conflicting case law and statutes.

HERE ARE THE FACTS THAT STAND OUT CONCERNING THE MODEL TERMINATION STATUTE:

First: There is a vital need for the statute at this time in nearly every one of the fifty states. Thousands of children and parents are adversely affected by the "hodge-podge" of confusing statutes and case law. Most trial judges simply have inadequate guidelines upon which to act. This is as true in Michigan as it is in all other states.

Second: After studying the statutes of the various states and other proposed model statutes, a simple conclusion emerges. The model statute written by the Neglected Children Committee is the best and most practical statute that has yet been devised to remedy this complex problem.

Third: Neither this, nor any other model statute, will ever be the last word on this complex problem, but if the fifty state legislatures were to adopt this model statute, verbatim, or in its essential wording, it would result in a greater measure of justice for thousands of children and parents. It would constitute a solid step forward in improving the juvenile justice system.

This model statute was not written as a doctoral thesis. The sole purpose of the project was to improve the quality of justice to children and their parents. You are strongly urged to take whatever steps are necessary to have the model act introduced as a bill and enacted into law by your state legislature.

For sixteen years I have served on committees that have written model acts, court rules, standards for juvenile courts, and so on. This project has given me the greatest sense of accomplishment and has been a new and wonderful experience. The committee that drafted this model act was well informed of the theories of behavioral science but tempered with insights which can only come from long experience of being responsible for making critical decisions in a courtroom.

Judges throughout America can present this model statute to their state legislatures with full confidence that the legislation that is proposed is a long step forward in achieving a greater measure of justice for the neglected children of America.

Judge James H. Lincoln, Chairman
Neglected Children Committee
National Council of Juvenile Court Judges

Editor's Note: Reprints of the Model Statute may be obtained by writing to: National Council of Juvenile Court Judges, Public Information Office, P.O. Box 8978, Reno, NV 89507.

Model Statute for Termination of Parental Rights

Unlike adults, who measure the passing of time by clocks and calendars, children have their own built-in time sense based on the urgency of their instinctual and emotional needs. What seems like a short wait to an adult can be an intolerable separation to a young child to whom a week can seem like a year and a month forever.

Children require stability and continuity in their care. The repeated uprooting of children who have been removed from their parental home and have developed environmental attachment to surrogate parents, is seriously detrimental to their physical, mental and emotional well-being.

It is the purpose of this act to delineate meaningful and clear guidelines to be applied to cases involving termination of parental rights.

To ensure the competent, stable, and ongoing care of the child by prompt and final adjudication, all orders and judgments of the Juvenile Court shall be affirmed on appeal unless the trial court committed a gross abuse of discretion, legal error to the substantial prejudice of the appellant, or the judgment is clearly and manifestly against the weight of the evidence. Appeals from an order terminating parental rights shall have precedence over all other cases in the Court to which the appeal is taken.

PERMANENT CUSTODY

SEC. 1

The purpose of this act is to provide a judicial process for the termination of all parental rights and responsibilities in situations set forth in this act; to delineate mandatory, but not exclusive, criteria for judicial consideration; to acknowledge that the time perception of children differs from that of adults; to pro-

vide stability in the lives of children who must be removed from their home and to make the ongoing needs of a child for proper physical, mental and emotional growth and development, the decisive considerations in permanent custody proceedings. Proceedings shall be civil in nature and governed by rules of civil procedure.

SEC. 2

(a) The Court of juvenile jurisdiction has exclusive and original jurisdiction to terminate the rights and responsibilities of parents of any child under 18 years of age found in the State for the reasons and circumstances set forth in Section 12.

(b) Where the Court has terminated the rights and responsibilities of parents, and has placed custody with a public or a private agency for adoptive placement, the Court shall, at least yearly, as long as the child remains unadopted, review the circumstances of the child to determine what efforts have been made to assure that the child has been adopted.

If the child has not been placed in a home for adoption, the Court may enter such orders as it deems necessary to further the adoption including placement with another agency.

SEC. 3 PETITION

(1) (a) The petition to terminate parental rights and all subsequent Court documents in the proceeding shall be subtitled "In the matter of _____ , a child." The petition shall be in writing and verified. The petition may be filed by a peace officer, Juvenile Court counselor, officer of the Court or employee of any public or private licensed child caring agency, or, with permission of the Court, by any interested person.

JAMES H. LINCOLN

(b) A petition filed by a peace officer, Juvenile Court counselor, officer of the Court, or employee of a public or private licensed child caring agency may be on information and belief of the petitioner. In all other cases the petition shall be on the personal knowledge of the petitioner.

(2) The petition shall set forth in ordinary and concise language such of the following facts as are known and indicate any which are not known:

(a) The name, age, and residence of child.

(b) The facts which bring the child within the jurisdiction of the Court as provided in Section 12.

(c) The name and residence of the child's parents, guardian, lawful custodian and person presently having physical custody of the child.

(d) That the petition is for the purpose of divesting all parental rights.

(e) The Court may for good cause suppress the address of any party.

SEC. 4 SUMMONS, ETC.

(1) Upon filing of the petition summons shall be issued forthwith on all persons required to be named in Sec. 3 (2) (c).

(2) A copy of the petition shall be attached to the summons in all cases other than service by publication. When served by publication, the notice shall contain a statement of the substance of the facts. All summons shall contain a statement to the effect that the hearing is for the purpose of terminating parental rights.

(3) The summons shall require the person or persons who have physical custody of the child to appear personally and bring the child before the Court at the time and place stated in the summons. Where, at the Court's discretion, it is deemed in the interest of the child that he need not be brought before the Court, the Court may so indicate. The summons shall be served at least 72 hours before the time set for the hearing and a copy of the petition shall be served together with the summons, and shall be made in the manner provided in the rules of civil procedure.

SEC. 5 SERVICE OF SUMMONS, ETC.

(1) Service of process shall be made according to the rules of civil procedure of the state.

SEC. 6 COMPLIANCE WITH SUMMONS

(1) If any person named in, and properly served with summons, shall without reasonable cause fail to appear or, when directed in the summons, to bring the child before the Court, then the Court may issue a bench warrant for such person, directing that he be taken into custody and brought before the Court.

(2) If the summons cannot be served or if the person to whom the summons is directed fails to obey it, the Court may issue an order to take the child into protective custody.

SEC. 7

(1) In any proceeding for terminating parental rights, or any rehearing or appeal thereon, the Court shall appoint an attorney to represent the child as his counsel and guardian ad litem.

(2) If the parent, or parents of the child desire to be represented by counsel but are indigent, the Court shall appoint an attorney for such parent or parents.

SEC. 8

(1) In all proceedings under this act the standard of proof to be adduced in all proceedings to terminate the rights and responsibilities of parents shall be a preponderance of the evidence

SEC. 9

(1) No doctor-patient privilege may be invoked with respect to hospital or medical records pertaining to any illness, trauma, incompetency, addiction to drugs or alcoholism of any parent.

SEC. 10

The record of the testimony of the parties adduced in any proceeding terminating parental rights and responsibilities to a child shall not be admissible in any civil, criminal

Model Statute for Termination of Parental Rights

or any other cause or proceedings in any Court against a person named as respondent for any purpose whatsoever, except in subsequent proceedings involving the same child or proceedings involving the same respondent, under the above sections.

Sec. 11

(1) The Court may conduct hearings in an informal manner and may adjourn the hearing from time to time. Stenographic notes or other verbatim reports of the hearing shall be taken and such record shall be stored as a permanent record of the Court.

Sec. 12 TERMINATION OF PARENTAL RIGHTS

(1) The Court may terminate parental rights when the Court finds the parent unfit or that the conduct or condition of the parent is such as to render him/her unable to properly care for the child and that such conduct or condition is unlikely to change in the foreseeable future. In determining unfitness, conduct or condition the Court shall consider, but is not limited to the following:

(a) Emotional illness, mental illness or mental deficiency of the parent, of such duration or nature as to render the parent unlikely to care for the ongoing physical, mental and emotional needs of the child.

(b) Conduct towards a child of a physically, emotionally or sexually cruel or abusive nature.

(c) Excessive use of intoxicating liquors or narcotic or dangerous drugs.

(d) Physical, mental or emotional neglect of the child.

(e) Conviction of a felony and imprisonment.

(f) Unexplained injury or death of a sibling.

(g) Reasonable efforts by appropriate public or private child caring agencies have been unable to rehabilitate the family.

(2) Where a child is not in the physical custody of the parent, the Court, in proceedings concerning the termination of parental rights, in addition to the foregoing, shall also consider, but is not limited to the following:

(a) Failure to provide care; or pay a reasonable portion of substitute physical care and maintenance where custody is lodged with others.

(b) Failure to maintain regular visitation or other contact with the child as designed in a plan to reunite the child with the parent.

(c) Failure to maintain reasonably consistent contact and/or communication with child.

(d) Lack of effort on the part of the parent to adjust his circumstances, conduct or conditions to meet the needs of the child.

(3) Where a child has been placed in foster care by a Court order or has been otherwise placed by parents or others into the physical custody of such family, the Court shall in proceedings concerning the termination of parental rights and responsibilities consider whether said child has become integrated into the foster family to the extent that his familial identity is with that family, and said family or person is able and willing to permanently so integrate the child. In such considerations, the Court shall note, but is not limited to the following:

(a) The love, affection and other emotional ties existing between the child and the parents, and his ties with the integrating family.

(b) The capacity and disposition of the parents from whom he was removed as compared with that of the integrating family to give the child love, affection and guidance and continuing the education of the child.

(c) The capacity and disposition of the parents from whom the child was removed and the integrating family to provide the child with food, clothing, medical care and other physical, mental and emotional needs.

(d) The length of time the child has lived in a stable, satisfactory environment and the desirability of maintaining such continuity.

(e) The permanence as a family unit of the integrating family or person.

(f) The moral fitness, physical and mental health of the parents from whom the child was removed and that of the integrating family or person.

JAMES H. LINCOLN

(g) The home, school and community record of the child, both when with the parents from whom he was removed and when with the integrating family.

(h) The reasonable preference of the child, if the Court deems the child of sufficient capacity to express a preference.

(i) Any other factor considered by the Court to be relevant to a particular placement of the child.

4. The rights of the parents may be terminated as provided herein if the Court finds that the parents have abandoned the child or the child was left under such circumstances that the identity of the parents is unknown and cannot be ascertained, despite diligent searching, and the parents have not come forward to claim the child within three months following the finding of the child.

(5) In considering any of the above basis for terminating the rights of a parent, the Court shall give primary consideration to the physical, mental or emotional condition and needs of the child.

Parents Ask Your Children. . .

Have you seen films like "The Lottery," "Future Shock," "The River" or "About Sex"?

Have you kept a journal or diary? (creative writing, english, etc.)

Have you written your obituary?

Have you had any classes dealing with TM or Witchcraft?

How often do you role-play? What characters do you take on?

How often do you discuss your family life in school?

Have you been in a magic circle?

Have you discussed alternate lifestyles? Have you discussed abortion?

How much of your school day is spent on *"The Basics"*?

Do you *stand* and *recite* the pledge of allegiance daily?

How often are you asked about your feelings?

Have you discussed a *"One World Government"*?

Have you read "The Learning Tree," "Pigman," "Forever" or "A Day No Pigs Would Die"?

Do you think our government should control industry?
Does the government owe you a job?
Has planned parenthood come in to speak to your class?
Have you been taken to a clinic?
Do your teachers ask you to make decisions about what is right and wrong?
Have you had the teacher read you your rights?
Have you been asked to determine ways to control the population?
Have you played "Dungeons & Dragons" in school?
Have you discussed personal things with your *teachers* and *counselors* and been told not to tell your parents, because they would not understand?
How often do you see your counselor?
Have you played survival games like, "The Bomb Shelter," "Domed City," or "Lifeboat"?
Have you ever played alligator river?

'Values Clarification — It's All Brainwashing!'

SOUTH ST. PAUL PUBLIC SCHOOLS
Special School District No. 6
South St. Paul, Minnesota 55075

TO: All Administrators

FROM: Ray I. Powell
Superintendent of Schools

RE: Center Bulletin No. 39 — 1974-75

DATE: February 26, 1975

1. Parents have the prime responsibility for the inculcation of those moral and spiritual values desired for their children in the areas of abortion and birth control. *Indeed, this is an inherent right of parents and must not be denied.*

Effective immediately, the teaching, advising, directing, suggesting, or counseling of students in these two (2) areas cannot be/shall not be the responsibility nor the task of the South St. Paul Public Schools.

Rather, the efforts of the public schools, henceforth, shall be directed towards expanding those complementary learning experiences in other areas of the total curriculum that will enhance these two (2) parental values, i.e.,

•preservation of the family unit.
•feminine role of wife, mother, and homemaker.
•masculine role of guide, protector, and provider.
•advocacy of home and family values.
•respect for family structure and authority.
•enhancement of womanhood and femininity.
•restoration of morality.

2. There are more and more concerns and questions being registered today regarding the questionable results and the true intent of SENSITIVITY TRAINING, as well as its germaneness to the goals and objectives of public education, the training of educators, and the learning experiences of students.

Consider these two (2) definitions of SENSITIVITY TRAINING (sources furnished upon request):

"Sensitivity training is defined as group meetings, large or small, to discuss publicly intimate and personal matters, and opinions, values or beliefs; and/or, to act out emotions and feelings toward one another in the group, using the techniques of self-confession and mutual criticism."

"It is also, 'coercive persuasion in the form of thought reform or brainwashing.'"

Consider, also, th t SENSITIVITY TRAINING by any other name is still *Sensitivity Train g*, as follows:

a. T-Group Training
b. Group Dynamic
c. Auto-Criticism
d. Operant Conditioning
e. Human Relations
f. Basic Encounter
g. Broad Sensitivity
h. Group Counseling
i. Management by Objectives
j. Self-Honest Session
k. Self-Examination
l. Interpersonal Competence
m. Interpersonal Relations

n. Self-Evaluation
o. Human Potential Workshop
p. Transactional Analysis (TA)
q. Group Criticism
r. Sex Education
s. Basic Sensuality
t. Self-Hypnosis
u. Humanizing Learning
v. Gestalt Psychosynthesis
w. Feeling Therapy
x. Role Playing
y. Psycho-Drama
z. Human Dynamics

aa. Values Clarification
bb. Teacher Effectiveness Training (TET)
cc. Leader Effectiveness Training
dd. Parent Effectiveness Training (PET)
ee. Youth Reaching — PEER
ff. Youth Reaching — TIES
gg. Couples Communication
hh. Situation Ethics
ii. Transcendental Meditation
jj. Self-Confession
kk. Away with Right and Wrong
ll. Group Consensus
mm. "New Morality"
nn. Away with "Ways of Elders"
pp. Innovative Process
qq. Identity Society
rr. Reality Therapy
ss. Schools Without Failure
tt. PPBS
uu. Psycho-Politics
vv. Behavioral Objectives
ww. Team Management
xx. Children's Ethics
yy. Team Teaching
zz. Alternative Life Styles

Is the prime concern in education today not to impart knowledge, but to change "attitudes," so that children can/will willingly accept a controlled society? Are the public schools being unwittingly reshaped to accomplish this and without realizing it?

A careful assessment is being undertaken over the next two (2) months to gather some answers to such questions as these. Staff members are invited to input to this co ation with any kind of information that is felt might be helpful.

RIPsgs

cc: Board Members
All Staff Members

APPENDIX D

WORLD OFFICE:
Suite 318, Atlantic Bldg.
930 F St. NW
Washington, DC 20004
USA
Tel: (202) 638-2662

JUDICIARY

World Court of Human Rights
Dr. Luis Kutner, Chief Justice
105 W. Adams Street
Chicago, Ill. 60603
(312) 782-1946

COMMISSIONS
(In formation)

Cultural
Yehudi Menuhin, Coordinator
London

Design-Science
Wm. Pork, Dep. Coordinator
Carbondale, IL

Forestry
Badi Lenz, Coordinator
Adel-Leeds, U.K.

Ocean
Edward R. Welles, Coordinator
Manset, ME

Space
Isaac Asimov, Coordinator
New York, NY
Carol S. Rosin
Deputy Coordinator
Clarksville, MD

WORLD POSTAL SERVICE
Washington, D.C. 20004

WORLD EDUCATION
Guru Nitya Chaitanya Yati
Narayana Gurukula
Srinivasapuram 695145
S. India

WORLD ECONOMICS
Norman Kurland
4318 North 31st St.
Arlington, VA 22207

World Government of World Citizens

Global Representation of Registered World Citizens
since 1953

I Basel   II London   III Washington, DC   IV Bauchi (Nig.)
V(a) Tel Aviv-Jaffa   V(b) Ammon   VIII Hong Kong   IX Colombo

ADMINISTRATION:
WORLD SERVICE
AUTHORITY
Garry Davis
Founder
World Coordinator

Dear Friend,

You are already a World Citizen in fact. By registering* as a citizen of the WORLD GOVERNMENT OF WORLD CITIZENS — which does not require giving up your nationality — you are joining a fast-growing sovereign constituency which has committed itself to establishing social, economic and political justice throughout the world in accordance with the fundamental moral codes of all major religions.

As a registered World Citizen, you have the opportunity to help evolve just and democratic WORLD LAWS, to be enacted eventually by an elected WORLD PARLIAMENT, administered by a WORLD EXECUTIVE, controlled by a WORLD COURT, and enforced by a WORLD PEACE FORCE.

From an economic world viewpoint, the gradual elimination of national armaments and the reconversion from scarcity thinking to abundance can transform our human community from one of increasing physical misery to individual and mutual prosperity. A World Citizen political party is in formation to help power these programs.

The WORLD GOVERNMENT OF WORLD CITIZENS in fact is already functioning in representing you and your needs on a global level. We issue WORLD PASSPORTS, WORLD CITIZEN CARDS, WORLD IDENTITY CARDS, and WORLD BIRTH CERTIFICATES, all in seven languages, and an intra-global postal service is beginning operations. These represent your *human* rights and are mandated by the Universal Declaration of Human Rights, approved by the General Assembly of the United Nations, 10 December 1948.

WORLD CITIZEN NEWS is the official journal of the WG of WC. Please subscribe. The brochure from the WORLD SERVICE AUTHORITY offers world citizenship literature to help you understand your new global commitment. To understand the origins and philosophy of the WG of WC, we urge you to send for the three basic documents: The Ellsworth Declaration, the Memorandum on World Government, and the 1978 Position Paper. My book, *My Country Is The World*, is also available.

The World Citizen Legal Fund is available to registered contributors to help defray their legal expenses in human rights violation cases. (See below).

I am looking forward to working together with you for a peaceful world under the CREDO OF A WORLD CITIZEN as stated on the back of this letter.

Yours in world service,

*See specimen card
on reverse side

Garry Davis

Fill out below and sign Pledge of Allegiance on reverse side and return with fee to:

APPLICATION FOR A WORLD CITIZEN REGISTRATION CARD

PLEASE PRINT OR TYPE ALL INFORMATION

SPECIMEN

FIRST NAME(S)		FAMILY NAME

BIRTHDATE | MONTH | YEAR | BIRTHPLACE

MALE | FEMALE | OCCUPATION
Telephone: Telex:
FOR OFFICIAL USE ONLY

WORLD CITIZEN REGISTRY NO.   WORLD PASSPORT NO.

WORLD ID CARD NO.   WORLD BIRTH CERTIFICATE NO.

MAIL WORLD CITIZEN CARD TO:

WORLD GOVERNMENT
OF WORLD CITIZENS
Suite 318, Atlantic Building
930 F Street, N.W.
Washington, D.C. 20004

One-time registration fee

Annual minimum financial commitment to WORLD GOVERNMENT programs on local, national, and global level and receive WORLD CITIZEN NEWS.

TOTAL

World Citizen Legal Fund
(Annual optional contribution)

Send check or money order

International Postal Reply Coupons also accepted. Exchange rate:
1 IRC = $.30

CREDO OF A WORLD CITIZEN

A World Citizen is a human being who lives intellectually, morally and physically in the present.

A World Citizen accepts the dynamic fact that the planetary human community is interdependent and whole, that humankind is essentially one.

A World Citizen is a peaceful and peacemaking individual, both in daily life and contacts with others.

As a global person, a World Citizen relates directly to humankind and to all fellow humans spontaneously, generously and openly. Mutual trust is basic to his/her life style.

Politically, a World Citizen accepts a sanctioning institution of representative government, expressing the general and individual sovereign will in order to establish and maintain a system of just and equitable world law with appropriate legislative, judiciary and enforcement bodies.

A World Citizen brings about better understanding and protection of different cultures, ethnic groups and language communities by promoting the use of a neutral international language, such as Esperanto.

A World Citizen makes this world a better place to live in harmoniously by studying and respecting the viewpoints of fellow citizens from anywhere in the world.

PLEDGE OF ALLEGIANCE

I, the undersigned, do hereby, willingly and consciously, declare myself to be a Citizen of the World. As a World Citizen, I pledge my planetary civic commitment to WORLD GOVERNMENT, founded on three universal principles of One Absolute Value, One World, and One Humanity which constitute the basis of World Law. As a World Citizen I acknowledge the WORLD GOVERNMENT as having the right and duty to represent me in all that concerns fundamental human rights and the General Good of human-kind and the Good of All.

As a Citizen of World Government, I affirm my awareness of my inherent responsibilities and rights as a legitimate member of the total world community of all men, women, and children, and will endeavor to fulfill and practice these whenever and wherever the opportunity presents itself.

As a Citizen of World Government, I recognize and re-affirm citizenship loyalties and responsibilities within the communal, state, and/or national groupings consistent with the principles of unity above which constitute now my planetary civic commitment.

_____

Signature of World Citizen

APPENDIX E

DEPARTMENT OF EDUCATION GRANTS FACT SHEET

HERE IS A PARTIAL LIST OF POLITICALLY LIBERAL ORGANIZATIONS WHO HAVE RECEIVED GRANTS FROM THE U.S. DEPARTMENT OF EDUCATION.

Organization	Date	Amount of Grant
American Friends Service Committee	June 30, 1981	$64,923
Bay Area Bilingual Education League	Sept. 30, 1982	$72,454
Council on Interracial Books For Children	July 1, 1981	$141,087
Federation of Southern Cooperatives	Sept. 25, 1981	$23,656
Feminist Press	July 2, 1981	$64,635
Feminist Press	July 30, 1981	$131,114
Institute for Labor Education Research	July 15, 1981	$99,933
International Ladies Garment Workers Union	July 31, 1981	$137,267
League of United Latin-American Citizens	May 31, 1981	$1,237,600
Mexican-American Legal Defense and Education Fund	June 25, 1981	$115,573
NOW Legal Defense & Education Fund	June 30, 1981	$170,178
NOW Legal Defense & Education Fund	Sept. 18, 1981	$105,577
National Student Educational Fund	February 27, 1981	$86,428
National Student Educational Fund (arm of United States Student Association)	June 25, 1981	$117,411
PUSH-EXCEL (Jesse Jackson)	September 30, 1981	$656,664
Planned Parenthood/San Francisco	August 1, 1981	$110,364
United States Student Association	July 31, 1981	$55,284
Urban Coalition	August 28, 1981	$46,935
Women's Action Alliance	June 30, 1981	$136,807
Working Women (National Association of Office Workers)	April 27, 1981	$82,202

American Taxpayers should not have to fund political causes, especially in the name of "education."

DIRECTION OF EDUCATION *Another viewpoint*

By Robert P. Dairon

In his book, "Behavior Control," Perry London reveals that, "Means are being found that will soon make possible precise control over much of people's individual actions, thoughts, emotions, moods and wills. Never in human history has this occurred before, except as fantasy."

Also, in 1969, the NEA (National Education Association), in a report "Education for the '70's And Beyond" stated: "Schools will become clinics whose purpose is to provide individuals. . . psychological treatment for the student, and teachers must become psychosocial therapists."

In the State of Maine today, more and more schools are using psychological techniques such as "Glasser's therapy programs," "values clarification" leading to behavior modification in all children, "health programs that are totally loaded with affective education, "drugs and alcohol" programs that seek to change the behavior of your children to "moderate" users.

"1984" is not far away; it is here now!

Our school children are being bombarded with affective education to a degree never encountered before in American education. An avalanche of federally-funded programs is being pushed on local school systems by state and federal agencies at an unprecedented rate, all under the humane consideration of "doing something for our needy children." Our State Department of Education is roaming the breadth and depth of the State of Maine urging school officials to use drug education programs that will—get this—teach children to use drugs and alcohol in moderation! Can you imagine a state agency, one that is spending public funds, offering school programs that will impart an attitude in school students of "It's OK to use drugs and alcohol as long as I use them wisely?"

Is it any wonder that we have seen such a tremendous increase in drug and alcohol abuse during the past decade? In order to stem this infusion of affective education, we need to ask some very simple questions: How much money has been spent in the State of Maine by the Department of Education during the '70's on drug abuse programs? What statistical results are available on (a) the number of students who were helped by these programs, (b) the number of students for whom the program did nothing? Do these programs in any way suggest "social acceptance" of responsible use of a small quantity of drugs? Will the program bring about and encourage a sympathetic attitude about drugs and drug abuse? Do parents want the schools to teach their children that "It is OK to use drugs, as long

Robert Dairon is a school administrator who lives in Rumford. He is curriculum director with 25 years of teaching experience. He is a member of the Board of Directors of Guardians of Education for Maine.

—*Bangor Daily News, Monday, February 11, 1980.*

Guardians of Education for Maine
P.O. Box 759, Camden, Maine 04843

as they are used moderately and wisely?" To a child who is on the fence about drug use, how can this type of suggestion help him ward off the feeling of using drugs? Do elementary school children have sufficient maturity and understanding for considering options? How can we be assured that the time spent on this program will yield definite and specific results? Why are we afraid to take a responsible and moral stand on drugs and alcohol?

Then, of course, we have the nasty business of schools prying and probing into the emotions and values of young elementary school children. Teachers' workshops buzz with talk of neurosis, resistance, maladjustment, workshops, teachers go blithely into the classrooms as "psychotherapists," arrange children in what is known as a Magic Circle and set up situations where ALL youngsters will reveal intimate feelings about themselves, their siblings, their parents and their peers; 'group confessionals" are set up where young children are subtly led to reveal details of routine peer infractions and, once revealed, permits the teacher to apply "psychological" punishments to children through the rationale of group consensus.

Children should not be exposed continually and sequentially to such devastating psychological persuasions; to do so will yield nothing in the long run, but passive maleable, docile and non-competitive young adults without individual personalities or inner strength.

Why are we allowing this psychrobable to permeate our schools? In fact, who gave the schools the authority to practice this technique of compulsory confession

with all children? If the schools have not mastered the job of teaching all children to read and write, why should we allow them to venture into the realm of mind-probing which, in itself, is so much more complicated than just plain teaching of the ABC's?

Presently, educators are concerned about the increasing trend in the growth of "Christian" schools throughout the country. The reason for this growth is very simple: Parents are sick and tired of seeing their schools turn into mental health clinics; parents are convinced that public schools foster an atmosphere that is completely secular, perhaps even antireligious. Please contemplate that for a period of time.

If present trends continue, public schools probably will in a few years hence, enroll mostly truants, dopeheads, alcoholics, failures, slow-learners, neurotics, special education crowd, unmotivated, alienated, etc. And just wait until you see the cost per pupil for this group! I, for one, am not enthusiastic about the prospect of schools becoming mental health clinics.

We—and that means all of us—need to re-examine the direction of education; we need to tell educators that the primary function of the schools is to develop intellectual capabilities, not probe little psyches; and we need to tell them that certain ethical, historical precepts will be taught in the schools in order that we might develop graduates who will understand the meaning of family, country, fidelity, honor and responsibility.

GEM takes a no-nonsense, basic approach to the education of Maine's young people.

Khrushchev Remembers

I suppose you could say my political education began during my boyhood in the little village of Kalinovka where I was born. My schoolteacher there was a woman named Lydia Shchevchenko. She was a revolutionary. She was also an atheist. She instilled in me my first political consciousness and began to counteract the effects of my strict religious upbringing. My mother was very religious, likewise her father — my grandfather — who as a serf had been conscripted into the tsarist army for twenty-five years. When I think back to my childhood, I can remember vividly the saints on the icons against the wall of our wooden hut, their faces darkened by fumes from the oil lamps. I remember being taught to kneel and pray in front of the icons with the grown-ups in church. When we were taught to read, we read the scriptures. But Lydia Shchevchenko set me on a path which took me away from all that.

Alert List for Humanist Programming

The difficulty in compiling an alert list is that humanist educationists have been infiltrating their ideas and techniques into the educational system for so long that they have completely displaced the traditional academic methods and curriculum. In addition, we have "bought into" their philosophy and methodology to such an extent that we find ourselves bankrupt for other ways to teach. I am forced to wonder if even among the retired teachers if there are many left who know the successful, prehumanist instructional procedures. In a sense, we are starting all over again.

The most important things to remember are the differences as to objectives. The humanists are interested in *conditioning, behavior modification,* and *values-free indoctrination.* Education is concerned with content and not with novelty entertainment. Knowledge is in itself rewarding despite humanist arguments to the contrary and relevance is not tied to a time element.

1) Avoid privacy invading activities, such as questionnaries, journals, diaries, data banks, family trees, and autobiographies.

2) Role playing and reversals, sociodramas and psychodramas, magic circles, group dynamics, sensitivity training, operant conditioning, etc., are dangerous methods which responsible psychiatrists have abandoned to effect behavior or attitudinal changes.

3) Problem solving and inquiry techniques. These procedures require that everything be questioned and subjected to "scientific" examination.

4) Decision making. This makes consensus the arbitor of right and wrong.

5) Thematic rather than chronological and factual studies in history for children introduce so much confusion that history is abandoned as irrelevant and dull.

6) Carefully scrutinize programs that stress the games and fun elements. Who shall survive games and games with open-ended questions are most obvious to avoid.

7) Closely evaluate high interest material dealing with space, such as, E.T., Close Encounters, Dungeons and Dragons, T.A., humanizing, valuing, situation ethics, alternate lifestyles, etc.

8) I recommend that you DO NOT teach comparative religions. Let Satan do his own work.

9) Do not accept at face value children's literature such as the Junior Book Program which are weekly readers.

I encourage you to concentrate on (1) preservation of the family as a two parent unit, (2) the feminine role as the wife, mother and homemaker, (3) the masculine role as husband, father and protector, (4) advocate and support the home and family values, and (5) re-enforce CHRISTIAN VALUES and their part in the creation of this nation.

The Teachings
of Humanism

ANALYSIS

Traditional Belief System of Bible (the law)	Comprehensive Belief System of Humanism
God, creation, morality the fallen state of man, and the free-enterprise system.	Humanism teaches – total hostile rejection of traditional beliefs and substitution of man, evolution, amorality, basic goodness of man, and one-world system in its place.
God has written His values (the Bible) and if man follows he will be prosperous and have life (love, joy, peace, patience,	Humanism teaches — Man to follow his own changing values and be responsible for the consequences of his actions (abortion, illegitimate

gentleness, kindness, dependability, goodness and self-control).

births, lesbianism, homosexuality, murder, hatred, strife, contention – in general – let it all hang out). Read Romans 1:22-32

God has made man in His image – spirit, soul and body to be in fellowship with Him.

Humanism teaches – Man is an animal (soul and body) and needs only to be rightly related with himself.

God is Supreme Being

Humanism denies existence of God.

God is Supreme Being, therefore faith and trust are in Him.

Humanism teaches Man is Supreme Being, therefore faith and trust is in man.

God does not change (there is certainty) therefore this system includes law which defines certainty.

Humanism teaches – there is *no certainty* because there is constant change (evolution) therefore law must be continually changed to the whims of man who is the Supreme Being.

God is a supernatural being, omnipotent (all powerful), omnipresent (present everywhere), omniscient (knowledge of everything).

Humanism teaches *psychic phenomena* to give man (Supreme Being) the sense (feeling) of being supernatural.

We have to ultimately answer directly to God for our actions.

Humanism teaches — the individual need answer only to himself. He is his own judge.

Life after Death

Denies life after death.

Lying is wrong

Lying is a relative term and therefore doesn't exist if the

	person thinks it is OK. (The end justifies the means).
There is a devil (Satan).	Denies existence of a devil (Satan).
God's name should not be profaned.	Humanism allows profaning God's name since it is just an expression. God does not exist.
Man is basically evil, separated from God and God has to determine a set of values for him.	Humanism teaches – Man is basically good and therefore is able to determine his own best values by himself.
The law is the authority that establishes the boundary of conduct.	Humanism teaches – no man need recognize any authority beyond himself.
God has freely given, (by grace) the law (so that we might not sin) and Jesus Christ (so that man can be reconciled by God).	Humanism teaches – there is no sin and man needs to be reconciled *only* to himself. (Self-actualization, self-realization).
Man is able to freely receive the benefits of God's grace by faith and enjoy all of its privileges.	Humanism teaches – Man's faith is in himself and he must stand up for his rights over and against others.
Where there is jealousy (suspicion) and strife there is disorder and every evil thing.	Humanism teaches – question the decisions of those in authority (teacher, parents) and role play strife and contention.
God has established an order, a framework, within which there is a governing authority which provides peace and tranquility.	Humanism teaches – Man's peace and tranquility is within himself and therefore he is his own authority.

Men and women are different.	Humanism teaches – men and women are the same.
The family is the basic unit of society. The family has responsibilities to fulfill physical necessities.	Humanism teaches – the individual is the basic unit of society. The society has responsibilities to fulfill the individual's physical necessities.
The legal age of majority is twenty-one years old.	Humanism teaches – a child is able to determine his own best values at any age. (Efforts are now being made to lower the age of statutory rape to 14 years old).
God is love.	Humanism teaches – sex is love.
Do unto others as you would have them do unto you. (Forgiveness is required here).	Humanism teaches – love is never having to say "I'm sorry". (No need for forgiveness).
Sex is for procreation and we are to multiply and inhabit the land.	Humanism teaches – we are over populated (a lie) and must stop having babies. (Zero population growth and Planned Parenthood)
Sex is a beautiful relationship between husband and wife who have become one flesh.	Sex is a physical animal need that must be gratified in any way that the person deems best.
The sovereignty of each nation to govern itself.	Humanism teaches – one-world system ruled by an intellectual elite. (The Humanists).
There are absolute rights	Humanism teaches – there

and wrongs, therefore:	are *no* absolute rights and wrongs, therefore:
A. Guilt and shame result when a person does something wrong (sin) according to that which is written (the law).	A. No guilt and shame exist because no one can do any wrong (sin). Wrong (sin) does not exist, therefore guilt and shame should not exist).
B. Forgiveness and/or punishment relieves guilt and shame.	B. No need for forgiveness and/or punishment.
Certain, absolute moral values: Incest is wrong.	Humanism teaches uncertain, amoral values: Incest is OK.
Prostitution is wrong.	Prostitution is OK.
Abortion-on-demand is wrong.	Abortion-on-demand is OK.
Homosexuality (sodomy) is wrong.	Homosexuality (sodomy) is OK.
Lesbianism (sodomy) is wrong.	Lesbianism (sodomy) is OK.
Sex outside marriage (fornication, adultery, etc.) is wrong.	Sex outside marrage (fornication, adultery, etc.) is OK.
Masturbation is wrong	Masturbation is OK.
Public nudity is wrong.	Public nudity is OK.
Sensuality and sexual intercourse should be in private.	Sensuality and sexual intercourse in public is OK.
Pornography is wrong.	Pornography is OK.
Use of drugs is wrong.	Use of drugs is OK. (Working to change narcotics laws).
Suicide is wrong.	Suicide is OK and is encouraged.

| Killing of old people and sick persons (euthanasia) is wrong. | Killing of old people and sick persons (euthanasia) is OK and is encouraged. |
| Masochism and sadism is wrong. | Masochism and sadism is OK. |

THIS IS BY NO MEANS THE COMPLETE LIST.

In *Humanist Magazine* (November/December 1980) author Riane Eisler says: "It is absurd to say. . . that one is a humanist but not a feminist. . . feminism is the last evolutionary development of humanism. Feminism is humanism on its most advanced level."

Riane Eisler wrote *The Equal Rights* (ERA) *Handbook.*

Karl Marx's own definition of Humanism reads: "Humanism is the denial of God, and the total affirmation of man. . . Humanism is really nothing else but Marxism." — *Karl Marx, Economic Politique et Philosophie,* Vol. I, pages 38-40.

"Soviet society today is the real embodiment of the ideas of proletarian, socialist humanism." — On The Policy of The Soviet Union and The International Situation by Leonid Brezhnev, prepared by the Novosti Press Agency Publishing House, Moscow — Doubleday & Company, Inc., Garden City, N.Y., 1973, page 27.

APPENDIX J

Humanist Manifestos
I and II

This contains the texts of Humanist Manifesto I and II as evidence of the anti-Christian beliefs of humanists and a preview of what America would be like if humanism were to be the religion of our people!

Humanist Manifesto I

   The time has come for widespread recognition of the radical changes in religious beliefs throughout the modern world. The time is past for mere revision of traditional attitudes. Science and economic change have disrupted the old beliefs. Religions the world over are under the necessity of coming to terms with new conditions created by a vastly increased knowledge and experience. In every field of human activity, the vital movement is now in the direction of a candid and explicit humanism. In order that religious humanism may be better understood we, the undersigned, desire to make certain affirmations which we believe the facts of our contemporary life demonstrate.

   There is great danger of a final, and we believe fatal, identification of the word *religion* with doctrines and methods which have lost their significance and which are powerless to solve the problem of human living in the Twentieth Century. Religions have always been means for realizing the highest values of life. Their end has been accomplished through the interpretation of the total environing situation (theology or world view), the sense of values resulting therefrom (goal or ideal), and the technique (cult) established for realizing the satisfactory life. A change in any of these factors results in alteration of the outward forms of religion. This fact explains the changefulness of religions through the centuries. But through all changes religion itself remains constant in its quest for abiding values, an inseparable feature of human life.

Today man's larger understanding of the universe, his scientific achievements, and his deeper appreciation of brotherhood, have created a situation which requires a new statement of the means and purposes of religion. Such a vital, fearless, and frank religion capable of furnishing adequate social goals and personal satisfactions may appear to many people as a complete break with the past. While this age does owe a vast debt to traditional religions, it is none the less obvious that any religion that can hope to be a synthesizing and dynamic force for today must be shaped for the needs of this age. To establish such a religion is a major necessity of the present. It is a responsibility which rests upon this generation . . .

First: Religious humanists regard the universe as self-existing and not created.

Second: Humanism believes that man is a part of nature and that he has emerged as the result of a continuous process.

Third: Holding an organic view of life, humanists find that the traditional dualism of mind and body must be rejected.

Fourth: Humanism recognizes that man's religious culture and civilization, as clearly depicted by anthropology and history, are the product of a gradual development due to his interaction with his natural environment and with his social heritage. The individual born into a particular culture is largely molded to that culture.

Fifth: Humanism asserts that the nature of the universe depicted by modern science makes unacceptable any supernatural or cosmic guarantees of human values. Obviously humanism does not deny the possibility of realities as yet undiscovered, but it does insist that the way to determine the existence and value of any and all realities is by means of intelligent inquiry and by the assessment of their relation to human needs. Religion must formulate its hopes and plans in the light of the scientific spirit and method.

Sixth: We are convinced that the time has passed for theism, deism, modernism, and the several varieties of "new thought."

Seventh: Religion consists of those actions, purposes, and experiences which are humanly significant. Nothing human is alien to the religious. It includes labor, art, science, philosophy, love, friendship, recreation — all that is in its degree expressive of intelligently satisfying human living. The distinction between the sacred and the secular can no longer be maintained.

Eighth: Religious humanism considers the complete realization of human personality to be the end of man's life and seeks its development and fulfillment in the here and now. This is the explanation of the humanist's social passion.

Ninth: In place of the old attitudes involved in worship and prayer the humanist finds his religious emotions expressed in a heightened sense of personal life and in a cooperative effort to promote social well-being.

Tenth: It follows that there will be no uniquely religious emotions and attitudes of the kind hitherto associated with belief in the supernatural.

Eleventh: Man will learn to face the crises of life in terms of his knowledge of their naturalness and probability. Reasonable and manly attitudes will be fostered by education and supported by custom. We assume that humanism will take the path of social and mental hygiene and discourage sentimental and unreal hopes and wishful thinking.

Twelth: Believing that religion must work increasingly for joy in living, religious humanists aim to foster the creative in man and to encourage achievements that add to the satisfactions of life.

Thirteenth: Religious humanism maintains that all associations and institutions exist for the fulfillment of human life. The intelligent evaluation, transformation, control, and direction of such associations and institutions with a view to the enhancement of human life is the purpose and program of humanism. Certainly religious institutions, their ritualistic forms, ecclesiastical methods, and communal activities must be reconstituted as rapidly as experience allows, in order to function effectively in the modern world.

Fourteenth: The humanists are firmly convinced that existing acquisitive and profit-motivated society has shown itself to be inadequate and that a radical change in methods, controls, and motives must be instituted. A socialized and cooperative economic order must be established to the end that the equitable distribution of the means of life be possible. The goal of humanism is a free and universal society in which people voluntarily and intelligently cooperate for the common good. Humanists demand a shared life in a shared world.

Fifteenth and last: We assert that humanism will: (a) affirm life rather than deny it; (b) seek to elicit the possibilities of life, not flee from it; and (c) endeavor to establish the conditions of a satisfactory life for all, not merely for the few. By this positive morale and intention humanism will be guided, and from this perspective and alignment the techniques and efforts of humanism will flow.

So stand the theses of religous humanism. Though we consider the religious forms and ideas of our fathers no longer adequate, the quest for the good life is still the central task for mankind. Man is at last becoming aware that he alone is responsible for the realization of the world of his dreams, that he has within himself the power for its achievement. He must set intelligence and will to the task.

J. A. C. Fagginer Auer	Bernard Fantus
E. Burdette Backus	William Floyd
Harry Elmer Barnes	F. H. Hankins
L. M. Birkhead	A. Eustace Haydon
Raymond B. Bragg	Llewellyn Jones
Edwin Arthur Burtt	Robert Morss Lovett
Ernest Caldecott	Harold P. Marley
A. J. Carlson	R. Lester Mondale
John Dewey	Charles Francis Potter
Albert C. Dieffenbach	John Herman Randall, Jr.
John H. Dietrich	Curtis W. Reese

HUMANIST MANIFESTO II (PREFACE)

It is forty years since Humanist Manifesto I (1933) appeared. Events since then make that earlier statement far too optimistic. Nazism has shown the depths of brutality of which humanity is capable. Other totalitarian regimes have suppressed human rights without ending poverty. Science has sometimes brought evil as well as good. Recent decades have shown that inhuman wars can be made in the name of peace. The beginnings of police states, even in democratic societies, widespread government espionage, and other abuses of power by military, political and industrial elites, and the continuance of unyielding racism, all present a different and difficult social outlook. In various societies, the demands of women and minority groups for equal rights effectively challenge our generation.

As we approach the twenty-first century, however, an affirmative and hopeful vision is needed. Faith, commensurate with advancing knowledge, is also necessary. In the choice between despair and hope, humanists respond in this Humanist Manifesto II with a positive declaration for times of uncertainty.

As in 1933, humanists still believe that traditional theism, especially faith in the prayer-hearing God, assumed to love and care for persons, to hear and understand their prayers and to be able to do something about them, is an unproven and outmoded faith. Salvationism based on mere affirmation, still appears as harmful, diverting people with false hopes of heaven hereafter. Reasonable minds look to other means for survival.

Those who sign Humanist Manifesto II disclaim that they are setting forth a binding credo; their individual views would be stated in widely varying ways. This statement is, however, reaching for vision in a time that needs direction. It is social analysis in an effort at consensus. New statements should be developed to supercede this, but for today it is our conviction that humanism offers an alternative that can serve present-day needs and guide humankind toward the future.

PAUL KURTS, *Editor*   EDWIN H. WILSON, *Editor Emeritus*
THE HUMANIST

HUMANIST MANIFESTO II

The next century can be and should be the humanistic century. Dramatic scientific, technological, and ever-accelerating social and political changes crowd our awareness. We have virtually conquered the planet, explored the moon, overcome the natural limits of travel and communication: we stand at the dawn of a new age; ready to move farther into space and perhaps inhabit other planets. Using technology wisely, we can control our environment, conquer poverty, markedly reduce disease, extend our lifespan, significantly modify our behavior, alter the course of human evolution and cultural development, unlock vast new powers, and provide humankind with unparalleled opportunity . . .

The future is, however, filled with dangers. In learning to apply the scientific method to nature and human life, we have opened the door to ecological damage, overpopulation, dehumanizing institutions, totalitarian repression, and nuclear and biochemical disaster. Faced with apocalyptic prophesies and doomsday scenarios, many flee in despair from reason and embrace irrational cults and theologies of withdrawal and retreat.

Traditional moral codes and newer irrational cults both fail to meet the pressing needs of today and tomorrow. False "theologies of hope" and messianic ideologies, substituting new dogmas for old, cannot cope with existing world realities. They separate rather than unite peoples.

Humanity, to survive, requires bold and daring measures. We need to extend the uses of scientific method, not renounce them, to fuse reason with compassion in order to build constructive social and moral values.

Confronted by many possible futures, we must decide which to pursue. The ultimate goal should be the fulfillment of the potential for growth in each human personality—not for the favored few, but for all of humankind. Only a shared world and global measures will suffice.

A humanist outlook will tap the creativity of each human being and provide the vision and courage for us to work together. This outlook emphasizes the role human beings can play in their own spheres of action. The decades ahead call for dedicated, clear-minded men and women able to marshal the will, intelligence, and cooperative skills for shaping a desirable future. Humanism can provide the purpose and inspiration that so many seek; it can give personal meaning and significance to human life.

Many kinds of humanism exist in the contemporary world. The varieties and emphases of naturalistic humanism include "scientific," "ethical," "democratic," "religious," and "Marxist" humanism. Free thought, atheism, agnosticism, skepticism, deism, rationalism, ethical culture, and liberal religion all claim to be heir to the humanist tradition. Humanism traces its roots from ancient China, classical Greece and Rome, through the Renaissance and the Enlightenment, to the scientific revolution of the modern world. But views that merely reject theism are not equivalent to humanism. They lack commitment to the positive belief in the possibilities of human progress and to the values central to it. Many within religious groups, believing in the future of humanism, now claim humanist credentials. Humanism is an ethical process through which we all can move, above and beyond the divisive particulars, heroic personalities, dogmatic creeds, and ritual customs of past religions or their mere negation.

We affirm a set of common principles that can serve as a basis for united action—positive principles relevant to the present human condition. They are a design for a secular society on a planetary scale.

For these reasons, we submit this new *Humanist Manifesto* for the future of humankind; for us, it is a vision of hope, a direction for satisfying survival.

RELIGION

First: In the best sense, religion may inspire dedication to the highest ethical ideals. The cultivation of moral devotion and creative imagination is an expression of genuine "spiritual" experience and aspiration.

We believe, however, that traditional dogmatic or authoritarian religions that place revelation, God, ritual, or creed above human needs and experience do a disservice to the human species. Any account of nature should pass the tests of scientific evidence; in our judgment, the dogmas and myths of traditional religions do not do so. Even at this late date in human history, certain elementary facts based upon the critical use of scientific reason have to be restated. *We find insufficient evidence for belief in the existence of a supernatural;* it is either meaningless or irrelevant to the question of the survival and fulfillment of the human race. *As non-theists, we begin with humans not God, nature not deity.* Nature may indeed be broader and deeper than we now know; any new discoveries, however, will but enlarge our knowledge of the natural.

Some humanists believe we should reinterpret traditional religions and reinvest them with meanings appropriate to the current situation. Such redefinitions, however, often perpetuate old dependencies and escapisms; they easily become obscurantist, impeding the free use of the intellect. We need, instead, radically new human purposes and goals.

We appreciate the need to preserve the best ethical teachings in the religious traditions of humankind, many of which we share in common. But *we reject those features of traditional religious morality that deny humans a full appreciation of their own potentialities and responsibilities. Traditional religions often offer solace to humans, but, as often, they inhibit humans from helping themselves* or experiencing their full potentialities. Such institutions, creeds, and rituals often impede the will to serve others. Too often traditional faiths encourage dependence rather than independence, obedience rather than affirmation, fear rather than courage. More recently they have generated concerned social action, with many signs of relevance appearing in the wake of the "God Is Dead" theologies. *But we can discover no divine purpose or providence for the human species.* While there is much that we do not know, *humans are responsible for what we are or will become. No deity will save us; we must save ourselves.*

Second: Promises of immortal salvation or fear of eternal damnation are both illusory and harmful. They distract humans from present concerns, from self-actualization, and from rectifying social injustices. Modern science discredits such historic concepts as the "ghost in the machine" and the "separable soul." Rather, science affirms that the human species is an emergence from natural evolutionary forces. As far as we know, the total personality is a function of the biological organism transacting in a social and cultural context. There is no credible evidence that life survives the death of the body. We continue to exist in our progeny and in the way that our lives have influenced others in our culture.

Traditional religions are surely not the only obstacles to human progress. Other ideologies also impede human advance. Some forms of political doctrine, for instance, function religiously, reflecting the worst features of orthodoxy and authoritarianism, especially when they sacrifice individuals on the altar of Utopian promises. Purely economic and political viewpoints, whether capitalist or communist, often function as religious and ideological dogma. Although humans undoubtedly need economic and political goals, they also need creative values by which to live.

ETHICS

Third: We affirm that moral values derive their source from human experience. Ethics is autonomous and situational, needing no theological or ideological sanction. Ethics stems from human need and interest. To deny this distorts the whole basis of life. Human life has meaning because we create and develop our futures. Happiness and the creative realization of human needs and desires, individually and in shared enjoyment, are continuous themes of humanism. We strive for the good life, here and now.

The goal is to pursue life's enrichment despite debasing forces of vulgarization, commercialization, bureaucratization, and dehumanization. *Fourth*: Reason and intelligence are the most effective instruments that humankind possesses. There is no subsitute; neither faith nor passion suffices in itself. The controlled use of scientific methods, which have transformed the natural and social sciences since the Renaissance, must be extended further in the solution of human problems. But reason must be tempered by humility, since no group has a monopoly of wisdom or virtue. Nor is there any guarantee that all problems can be solved or all questions answered. Yet critical intelligence, infused by a sense of human caring, is the best method that humanity has for resolving problems. Reason should be balanced with compassion and empathy and the whole person fulfilled. Thus, we are not advocating the use of scientific intelligence independent of or in opposition to emotion, for we believe in the cultivation of feeling and love. As science pushes back the boundary of the known, man's sense of wonder is continually renewed, and art, poetry, and music find their places, along with religion and ethics.

THE INDIVIDUAL

Fifth: The preciousness and dignity of the individual person is a central humanist value. Individuals should be encouraged to realize their own creative talents and desires. We reject all religious, ideological, or moral codes that denigrate the individual, suppress freedom, dull intellect, dehumanize personality. We believe in maximum individual autonomy consonant with social responsibility. Although science can account for the causes of behavior, the possibilities of individual freedom of choice exist in human life and should be increased.

Sixth: In the area of sexuality, we believe that intolerant attitudes, often cultivated by orthodox religions and puritanical cultures, unduly repress sexual conduct. The right to birth control, abortion, and divorce should be recognized. While we do not approve of exploitive, denigrating forms of sexual expression, neither do we wish to prohibit, by law or social sanction, sexual behavior between consenting adults. The many varieties of sexual exploration should not in themselves be considered "evil." Without countenancing mindless permissiveness or unbridled promiscuity, a civilized society should be a tolerant one. Short of harming others or compelling them to do likewise, individuals should be permitted to express their sexual proclivities and pursue their life-styles as they desire. We wish to cultivate the development of a responsible attitude toward sexuality, in which humans are not exploited as sexual objects, and in which intimacy, sensitivity, respect, and honesty in interpersonal relations are encouraged. Moral education for children and adults is an important way of developing awareness and sexual maturity.

DEMOCRATIC SOCIETY

Seventh: To enhance freedom and dignity the individual must experience a full range of *civil liberties* in all societies. This includes freedom of speech and the press, political democracy, the legal right of opposition to governmental policies, fair judicial process, religious liberty, freedom of association, and artistic, scientific, and cultural freedom. It also includes a recognition of an individual's right to die with dignity, euthanasia, and the right to suicide. We oppose the increasing invasion of privacy, by whatever means, in both totalitarian and democratic societies. We would safeguard, extend, and implement the principles of human freedom evolved from the *Magna Carta* to the *Bill of Rights*, the *Rights of Man,* and the *Universal Declaration of Human Rights.*

Eighth: We are committed to an open and democratic society. We must extend participatory democracy in its true sense to the economy, the school, the family, the workplace, and voluntary associations. Decision-making must be decentralized to include widespread involvement of people at all levels—social, political, and economic. All persons should have a voice in developing the values and goals that determine their lives. Institutions should be responsive to expressed desires and needs. The conditions of work, education, devotion, and play should be humanized. Alienating forces should be modified or eradicated and bureaucratic structures should be held to a minimum. People are more important than decalogues, rules, proscriptions, or regulations.

Ninth: The separation of church and state and the separation of ideology and state are imperatives. The state should encourage maximum freedom for different moral, political, religious, and social values in society. It should not favor any particular religious bodies through the use of public monies, nor espouse a single ideology and function thereby as an instrument of propaganda or oppression, particularly against dissenters.

Tenth: Humane societies should evaluate economic systems not by rhetoric or ideology, but by whether or not they increase economic well-being for all individuals and groups, minimize poverty and hardship, increase the sum of human satisfaction, and enhance the quality of life. Hence the door is open to alternative economic systems. We need to democratize the economy and judge it by its responsiveness to human needs, testing results in terms of the common good.

Eleventh: The principle of moral equality must be furthered through elimination of all discrimination based upon race, religion, sex, age, or national origin. This means equality of opportunity and recognition of talent and merit. Individuals should be encouraged to contribute to their own betterment. If unable, then society should provide means to satisfy their basic economic, health, and cultural needs, including, wherever resources make possible, a minimum guaranteed annual income. We are concerned for the welfare of the aged, the infirm, the disadvantaged, and also for the outcasts—the mentally retarded, abandoned, or abused children, the handicapped, prisoners, and addicts—for *all* who are neglected or ignored by society. Practicing humanists should make it their vocation to humanize personal relations.

We believe in the *right to universal education.* Everyone has a right to the cultural opportunity to fulfill his or her unique capacities and talents. The schools should foster satisfying and productive living. They should be open at all levels to any and all, the achievement of excellence should be encouraged. Innovative and experimental forms of education are to be welcomed. The energy and idealism of the young deserve to be appreciated and channeled to constructive purposes.

We deplore racial, religious, ethnic, or class antagonisms. Although we believe in cultural diversity and encourage racial and ethnic pride, we reject separations which promote alienation and set people and groups against each other; we envision an *integrated* community where people have a maximum opportunity for free and voluntary association.

We are *critical of sexism or sexual chauvinism*—male or female. We believe in equal rights for both women and men to fulfill their unique careers and potentialities as they see fit, free of invidious discrimination.

WORLD COMMUNITY

Twelfth: We deplore the division of humankind on nationalistic grounds. We have reached a turning point in human history where the best option is to *transcend the limits of national sovereignty* and to move toward the building of a world community in which all sectors of the human family can participate. Thus we look to the development of a system of world law and a world order based upon transnational federal government. This would appreciate cultural pluralism and diversity. It would not exclude pride in national origins and accomplishments nor the handling of regional problems on a regional basis. Human progress, however, can no longer be achieved by focusing on one section of the world. Western or Eastern, developed or underdeveloped, for the first time in human history, no part of humankind can be isolated from any other. Each person's future is in some way linked to all. We thus reaffirm a commitment to the building of world community, at the same time recognizing that this commits us to some hard choices.

Thirteenth: This world community must *renounce the resort to violence and force* as a method of solving international disputes. We believe in the peaceful adjudication of differences by international courts and by the development of the arts of negotiation and compromise. War is obsolete. So is the use of nuclear, biological, and chemical weapons. It is a planetary imperative to reduce the level of military expenditures and turn these savings to peaceful and people-oriented uses.

Fourteenth: The world community must engage in *cooperative planning* concerning the use of rapidly depleting resources. The planet earth must be considered a single *ecosystem*. Ecological damage, resource depletion, and excessive population growth must be checked by international concord. The cultivation and conservation of nature is a moral value; we should perceive ourselves as integral to the sources of our being in nature. We must free our world from needless pollution and waste, responsibly guarding and creating wealth, both natural and human. Exploitation of natural resources, uncurbed by social conscience, must end.

Fifteenth: The problems of *economic growth and development* can no longer be resolved by one nation alone; they are worldwide in scope. It is the moral obligation of the developed nations to provide—through an international authority that safeguards human rights—massive technical, agricultural, medical, and economic assistance, including birth control techniques, to the developing portions of the globe. World poverty must cease. Hence extreme disproportions in wealth, income, and economic growth should be reduced on a worldwide basis.

Sixteenth: Technology is a vital key to human progress and development. We deplore any neo-romantic efforts to condemn indiscriminately all technology and science or to counsel retreat from its further extension and use for the good of humankind. We would resist any moves to censor basic scientific research on moral, political, or social grounds. Technology must, however, be carefully judged by the consequences of its use; harmful and destructive changes should be avoided. We are particularly disturbed when technology and bureaucracy control, manipulate, or modify human beings without their consent. Technological feasibility does not imply social or cultural desirability.

Seventeenth: We must expand communication and transportation across frontiers. Travel restrictions must cease. The world must be open to diverse political, ideological, and moral viewpoints and evolve a worldwide system of television and radio for information and education. We thus call for full international cooperation in culture, science, the arts, and technology *across ideological borders*. We must learn to live openly together or we shall perish together.

HUMANITY AS A WHOLE

In closing: The world cannot wait for a reconciliation of competing political or economic systems to solve its problems. These are the times for men and women of good will to further the building of a peaceful and prosperous world. We urge that parochial loyalties and inflexible moral and religious ideologies be transcended. We urge recognition of the common humanity of all people. We further urge the use of reason and compassion to produce the kind of world we want—a world in which peace, prosperity, freedom, and happiness are widely shared. Let us not abandon that vision in despair or cowardice. We are responsible for what we are or will be. Let us work together for a humane world by means commensurate with humane ends. Destructive ideological differences among communism, capitalism, socialism, conservatism, liberalism, and radicalism should be overcome. Let us call for an end to terror and hatred. We will survive and prosper only in a world of shared humane values. We can initiate new directions for humankind; ancient rivalries can be superseded by broad-based cooperative efforts. The commitment to tolerance, understanding, and peaceful negotiation does not necessitate acquiescence to the status quo nor the damming up of dynamic and revolutionary forces. The true revolution is occurring and can continue in countless non-violent adjustments. But this entails the willingness to step forward onto new and expanding plateaus. At the present juncture of history, commitment to all humankind is the highest commitment of which we are capable; it transcends the narrow allegiances of church, state, party, class, or race in moving toward a wider vision of human potentiality. What more daring a goal for humankind than for each person to become, in ideal as well as practice, a citizen of a world community. It is a classical vision; we can now give it new vitality. Humanism thus interpreted is a moral force that has time on its side. We believe that humankind has the potential intelligence, good will, and cooperative skill to implement this commitment in the decades ahead.

We, the undersigned, while not necessarily endorsing every detail of the above, pledge our general support to Humanist Manifesto II for the future of humankind. These affirmations are not a final credo or dogma but an expression of a living and growing faith. We invite others in all lands to join us in further developing and working for these goals.

Lionel Abel, *Prof. of English, State Univ. of New York at Buffalo*
Khoren 'Arisian, *Board of Leaders. NY Soc. for Ethical Culture*
Isaac Asimov, *author*
George Axtelle, *Prof. Emeritus. Southern Illinois Univ.*
Archie J. Bahm, *Prof. of Philosophy Emeritus. Univ. of N.M.*
Paul H. Beattie, *Pres., Fellowship of Religious Humanists*
Keith Heggs, *Exec. Dir., American Humanist Association*
Malcolm Bissell, *Prof. Emeritus. Univ. of Southern California*
H. J. Blackham, *Chm., Social Morality Council. Great Britain*
Brand Blanshard, *Prof. Emeritus. Yale Univ.*
Paul Blanshard, *author*
Joseph L. Blau, *Prof. of Religion. Columbia Univ.*
Sir Hermann Bondi, *Prof. of Math., King's Coll., Univ. of London*
Howard Box, *Leader. Brooklyn Soc. for Ethical Culture*
Raymond B. Bragg, *Minister Emeritus., Unitarian Ch., Kansas City*
Theodore Brameld, *Visiting Prof., C.U.N.Y.*
Brigid Brophy, *author. Great Britain*
Lester R. Brown, *Senior Fellow. Overseas Development Council*
Bette Chambers, *Pres., American Humanist Association*
John Ciardi, *poet*
Francis Crick, *M. D., Great Britain*
Arthur Danto, *Prof. of Philosophy. Columbia Univ.*
Lucien de Coninck, *Prof., University of Gund. Belgium*
Miriam Allen deFord, *author*
Edd Doerr, *Americans United for Separation of Church and State*
Peter Draper, *M. D., Guy's Hospital Medical School, London*
Paul Edwards, *Prof. of Philosophy. Brooklyn College*
Albert Ellis, *Exec. Dir., Inst. Adv. Study Rational Psychotherapy*
Edward L. Ericson, *Board of Leaders. NY Soc. for Ethical Culture*
H. J. Eysenck, *Prof. of Psychology. Univ. of London*
Roy P. Fairfield, *Coordinator. Union Graduate School*
Herbert Feigl, *Prof. Emeritus, Univ. of Minnesota*
Raymond Firth, *Prof. Emeritus of Anthropology. Univ. of London*
Antony Flew, *Prof. of Philosophy. The Univ.., Reading, England*
Kenneth Furness, *Exec. Secy., British Humanist Association*
Erwin Gaede, *Minister. Unitarian Church. Ann Arbor, Mich.*
Richard S. Gilbert. *Minister. First Unitarian Ch., Rochester, N.Y.*
Charles Wesley Grady, *Minister. Unit. Univ. Ch., Arlington, Ma.*
Maxine Greene, *Teachers College, Columbia Univ.*
Thomas C. Greening, *Editor, Journal of Humanistic Psychology*
Alan F. Guttmacher, *Pres., Planned Parenthood Fed. of America*
J. Harold Hadley, *Minister. Unit. Univ. Ch., Pt. Washington, N. Y.*
Hector Hawton, *Editor. Question, Great Britain*
A. Eustace Haydon, *Prof. Emeritus of History of Religions*
James Hemming. *Psychologist. Great Britain*
Palmer A. Hilty. *Adm. Secy., Fellowship of Religious Humanists*
Hudson Hoagland, *Pres. Emeritus. Worcester Fdn. for Exper. Bio.*

Robert S. Hoagland. *Editor,* Religious Humanism
Sidney Hook, *Prof. Emeritus of Philosophy, New York Univ.*
James F. Hornbock, *Leader, Ethical Soc. of St. Louis*
James M. Hutchinson, *Minister Emeritus. First Unit. Ch., Cincinnati*
Mordecai M. Kaplan, *Rabbi. Fndr. of Jewish Reconstr. Movement*
John C. Kidnergn, *Prof. of Social Work., Univ. of Minnesota*
Lester A. Kirkendall, *Prof. Emeritus, Oregon State Univ.*
Margaret Knight, *Univ. of Aberdeen. Scotland*
Jean Kotkin, *Exec. Secy., American Ethica Union*
Richard Kostelanets, *poet*
Paul Kurtz, *Editor.* The Humanist
Lawrence Lader. *Chm., Natl. Assn. for Repeal of Abortion Laws*
Edward Lamb. *Pres., Lamb Communications, Inc.*
Corliss Lamont, *Chm., Natl. Emergency Civil Liberties Union*
Chauncey D. Leake, *Prof., Univ. of California. San Francisco*
Alfred McC. Lee, *Prof. Emeritus, Soc. Anthropology, C.U.N.Y.*
Elizabeth Briant Lee, *author*
Christopher Macy, *Dir., Rationalist Press Assn., Great Britain*
Clorinda Margolis, *Jefferson Comm. Mental Health Cen., Phila.*
Joseph Margolis, *Prof. of Philosophy. Temple Univ.*
Harold P. Marley, *Ret. Unitarian Minister*
Floyd W. Matson, *Prof. of American Studies. Univ. of Hawaii*
Lester Mondale, *former Pres., Fellowship of Religious Humanists*
Lloyd Morain, *Pres., Illinois Gas Company*
Mary Morain, *Editorial BJ., Intl. Soc. for General Semantics*
Charles Morris, *Prof. Emeritus. Univ. of Florida*
Henry Morgentaler, *M. D., Past Pres., Humanist Assn. of Canada*
Mary Mothersill, *Prof. of Philosophy, Barnard College*
Jerome Nathanson, *Chem., Bd. of Leaders, NY Soc. Ethical Culture*
Billy Joe Nichols, *Minister, Richardson Unitarian Church. Texas*
Kai Nielsen, *Prof. of Philosophy. University of Calgary, Canada*
P. H. Nowell-Smith, *Prof. of Philosophy, York Univ., Canada*
Chaim Perelman, *Prof. of Philosophy. Univ. of Brussels. Belgium*
James W. Prescott, *Natl. Inst. of Child Health and Human Dev.*
Harold J. Quigley, *Leader, Ethical Humanist Society of Chicago*
Howard Radest, *Prof. of Philosophy, Ramapo College*
John Herman Randall, Jr., *Prof. Emeritus, Columbia Univ.*
Oliver L. Reiser, *Prof. Emeritus. Univ. of Pittsburgh*
Lord Ritchie-Calder, *formerly Univ. of Edinburgh. Scotland*
B. T. Rocca, Jr., *Consultant, Intl. Trade and Commodities*
Andrei D. Sakharov, *Academy of Sciences. Moscow. U.S.S.R.*
Sidney H. Scheuer, *Chm.. Natl. Comm. for an Effective Congress*
Herbert W. Schneider, *Prof. Emeritus. Claremont Grad. School*
Clinton Lee Scott, *Universalist Minister. St. Petersburgh, Fla.*
Roy Wood Sellars, *Prof. Emeritus, University of Michigan*
A. B. Shah, *Pres. Indian Secular Society*
B. F. Skinner, *Prof. of Psychology, Harvard Univ.*
Kenneth J. Smith, *Leader, Philadelphia Ethical Society*
Matthew Ies Spetter, *Chm., Dept. Ethics. Ethical Culture Schools*
Mark Starr, *Chm. Esperanto Info. Center*
Svetozar Stojanovic, *Prof. Philosophy, Univ. Belgrade. Yogoslavia*
Harold Taylor, *Project Director, World University Student Project*
V. T. Thayer, *author*
Herbert A. Tonne, *Ed. Board.* Journal of Business Education
Jack Tourin, *Pres., American Ethical Union*
E. C. Vanerlaan, *lecturer*
J. P. van Praag, *Chem., Intl. Humanist and Ethical Union, Utrecht*
Maurice B. Visscher, *M. D., Prof. Emeritus. Univ. of Minnesota*
Goodwin Watson, *Assn. Coordinator. Union Graduate School*
Gerald Wendt, *author*

Henry N. Wieman, *Prof. Emeritus. Univ. of Chicago*
Sherwin Wine, *Rabbi. Soc. for Humanistic Judaism*
Edwin H. Wilson, *Ex. Dir. Emeritus. American Humanist Assn.*
Bertram D. Wolfe, *Hoover Institution*
Alexander S. Yesenin Volpin, *mathematician*
Marvin Zimmerman, *Prof. of Philosophy. State Univ. NY at Bib.*

BANGLADESH:

Abul Hasanat, *Secretary, Bangladesh Humanist Society*

CANADA:

J. Lloyd Brereton, *ed., Humanist in Canada*
Andrew Malleson, M.D. *psychiatrist*
Eleanor Wright Peirine, *author*
Bernard Porter, *Pres., Toronto Humanist Assn.*

FRANCE:

Pierre Lamarque
Jacques Monod, *Institut Pasteur*
Jean-Francois Revel, *journalist*

GERMANY (WEST):

Walter Behrendt, *Vice Pres., European Parliament*
W. Bonness, *Pres., Bund Freirelgioser Gemeinden*
D. Bronder, *Bund Freirelgioser Gemeinden*

GREAT BRITAIN:

Sir Alfred Ayer, *Prof., Oxford*
Sir Julian Huxley, *former hd., UNESCO*

INDIA:

G. D. Parikh, *Indian Radical Humanist Assn.*
A. Solomon, *coordinator, Indian Secular Society*
V. M. Tarkunde, *Pres., All Indian Radical Humanist Assn.*

NIGERIA:

Ernest N. Ukpaby, *Dean. Univ. of Nigeria*

PHILIPPINES:

Gonzalo Quiogue, *Vice Pres., Humanist Assn. of the Philippines*

SOVIET UNION:

Zhores Medvedev, *scientist*

SWEDEN:

Gunnar Myrdal, *Prof. Univ. of Stockholm*

U. S. A.:

Gina Allen, *author*
John C. Anderson, *Humanist Counselor*
Peter O. Anderson, *Asst. Prof., Ohio State Univ.*
William F. Anderson, *Humanist Counselor*

John Anton, *Prof., Emory University*
Celia Baker
Ernest Baker, *Assoc. Prof., Univ. of the Pacific*
Marjorie S. Baker, Ph. D., *Pres., Humanist Community of San Francisco*
Henry S. Basayne, *Assoc. Exec. Officer, Assn. for Humanistic Psychology*
Mildred H. Blum, *Sec'y., American Ethical Union*
Robert O. Boothe, *Prof. Emer., Cal. Polytechnic*
Clement A. Bosch
Madeline L. Bosch
Bruni Boyd, *Vice Pres., American Ethical Union*
Nancy Brewer, *Humanist Counselor*
Charles Brownfield, *Asst. Prof., Queensborough Community College, CUNY*
Constantia Brownfield, *R. N.,*
Margaret Brown, *Assoc. Prof., Oneonta State Univ. College*
Beulah L. Bullard, *Humanist Counselor*
Joseph Chuman, *Leader, Ethical Soc. of Essex Co.*
Gordon Clanton, *Asst. Prof., Trenton State College*
Daniel S. Collins, *Leader, Unitarian Fellowship of Jonesboro, Ark.*
Wm. Creque, *Pres., Fellowship of Humanity, Oakland, Ca.*
M. Benjamin Dell, *Dir. Amer. Humanist Assn.*
James Durant IV, *Prof., Polk Comm. College, Winter Haven, Fla.*
Gerald A. Ehrenreich, *Assoc. Prof., Univ. of Kansas School of Medicine*
Marie Erdmann, *Teacher, Campbell Elem. Sch.*
Robert L. Erdmann, *Ph.D., IBM*
Hans S. Falck, *Disting. Prof., Menninger Fdn*
James Farmer, *Dir. Public Policy Training Inst.*
Ed Farrar
Joe Felmet, *Humanist Counselor*
Thomas Ferrick, *Leader, Ethical Soc. of Boston*
Norman Fleishman, *Exec. Vice Pres., Planned Parenthood World Population, Los Angeles*
Joseph Fletcher, *Visiting Prof., Sch. of Medicine, Univ. of Virginia*
Douglas Frazier, *Leader, American Ethical Union*
Betty Friedan, *Founder, N. O. W.*
Harry M. Geduold, *Prof., Indiana University*
Roland Gibson, *Pres., Art Fdn. of Potsdam, N. Y.*
Aron S. Gilmartin, *Minister, Mt. Diablo Unitarian Church, Walnut Creek, Ca.*
Annabelle Glasser, *Dir., Amer. Ethical Union*
Rebecca Goldblum, *Dir. Amer. Ethical Union*
Louis R. Gomberg, *Humanist Counselor*
Harold N. Gordon, *Vice Pres., Amer. Ethical Univ.*
Sol Gordon, *Prof., Syracuse University*
Theresa Gould, *American Ethical Union*
Gregory O. Grant, *Captain, USAF*
Ronald Green, *Asst. Prof., New York Univ.*
LeRue Grim, *Secretary, Amer Humanist Assn.*
S. Spencer Grin, *Pub., Saturday Review/World*
Josephine R. Gurgard, *Sec'y. Humanist Society of Greater Philadelphia*
Samuel J. Gurbarg
Lewis M. Gubrud, *Exec. Dir., Mediator Fellowship, Providence, R.I.*
Frank A. Hall, *Minister, Murray Univ. Church, Attleboro, Mass.*
Harold Hansen, *Pres., Space Coast Chapter, AHA*
Ethelbert Haskins, *Dir., Amer. Humanist Assn.*
Lester H. Hayes, *Public Relations Dir., American Income Life Insurance Co.*
Donald E. Henshaw, *Humanist Counselor*
Alex Hershaft, *Principal Scientist, Booz Allen Applied Research*
Ronald E. Hestand, *author and columnist*
Irving Louis Horowitz, *editor,* Society
Warren S. Hoskins, *Humanist Counselor*
Mark W. Huber, *Director, Amer. Ethical Union*

Harold J. Hutchison, *Humanist Counselor*
Arthur M. Jackson, *Exec. Dir., Humanist Comm.,San Jose; Treasurer, Amer. Humanist Assn.*
Linda R. Jackson, *Dir., Amer. Humanist Assn.*
Steven Jacobs, *former Pres., Amer. Ethical Union*
Thomas B. Johnson, Jr., *consulting psychologist*
Robert Edward Jones, *Exec. Dir., Joint Washington Office for Social Concern*
Marion Kahn, *Pres., Humanist Society of Metropolitan New York*
Alec E. Kelley, *Prof., Univ. of Arizona*
Marvin Kohl, *Prof., SUNY at Fredonia*

APPENDIX K
Bibliography

1) Cotter, John, *A Study in Syncretism*, Canadian Intelligence Publications, 1983.
2) Corti, Count Egon Ceasar, *The Rise of the House of Rothschild*, Western Islands, 1972.
3) Deyo, Stan, *The Cosmic Conspiracy*, WATT, 1978.
4) Marx, Karl, *The Communist Manifesto*, American Opinion Press, 1974.
5) Nesbitt, Vince, *Humanistic Morals and Values Education*, N.S.W. 2066 Australia.
6) Norris, Dr. Murray, *Weep for your Children*, Box 73, Clovis, CA 93661.3.
7) Smith, Bernard, *Approaches* Magazine, August 1974.
8) Sutton, Anthony, *How the Order Controls Education*, Research Publication, 1983.
9) Taylor, Paula, *The Kids' Whole Future Catalogue*, Random House, 1982.
10) Whitehead, John W., *The Stealing of America*, Crossway Books, Illinois, 1983.
11) Winrod, Gerald, *Adam Weishaupt*, Emmissary Publications, 1937.
12) Wright, Erminie K., *The Conquest of Democracy*, Educational Research Bureau, no date.

FOR FURTHER READING AND
LISTENING WE RECOMMEND:

_____ OUR SPECIAL EDUCATION PACKET $5.00
_____ *CHANGE AGENTS IN THE SCHOOLS*
by Barbara Morris $10.00
_____ *WHY ARE YOU LOSING YOUR
CHILDREN* by Barbara Morris $5.00
_____ *TUITION TAX CREDITS*
by Barbara Morris $6.00
_____ *CONQUEST OF DEMOCRACY*
by Erminie King Wright $4.00
_____ *STEALING OF AMERICA*
by John Whitehead $6.95
_____ *FREEDOM OF RELIGIOUS EXPRESSION
IN THE PUBLIC SCHOOLS* $3.95
_____ *NEBRASKA PACKET–RELIGIOUS FREEDOM
–HAVE WE LOST IT?* $2.50
_____ HUMANISTIC MORALS AND VALUES
EDUCATION by Vince Nesbitt $3.00
_____ *TRACS NEWSLETTER* by William Bowen
and Sandy McKasson $1.50
_____ *HERO NEWSLETTER* ON "THE NEW AGE" $1.50

_____ "WHAT DO I DO NOW?"
by Penny Bowen $5.00
_____ "Freedom In Education"
by Jacqualine Lawrence $5.00
_____ "Parent Advocates" by Laura Rodgers $5.00
_____ "Our Children Are Being Programmed"
by Dr. J. Bean $5.00
_____ "Who Has The Children"
by Sandy McKasson (2 tapes) $12.00
_____ "Jailed For His Faith"
by Rev. Everett Sileven $5.00
_____ "Christian Resistance" by Rev. Sileven $5.00
_____ "Biblical Principles Of Government"
by Rev. Sileven $5.00
_____ "American Government As It Was Intended"
by Rev. Sileven $5.00

The above information may be ordered directly from HERO. Make check payable to *HERO* and include $1.50 for postage for each $10.00 order. Send to *HERO*, P. O. Box 202, Jarrettsville, Md. 21084. WE ARE *NOT* A TAX EXEMPT CORPORATION. We do receive donations for our work and covet your prayers.

OTHER NEWSLETTERS TO WRITE FOR:

Barbara Morris Report, P. O. Box 756, Upland, CA 91786
Pro-Family Forum Alert, P. O. Box 8907, 3601 E. Lancaster, Ft. Worth, TX 76112
WATCH, Box 5, Harmons, MD 21077
Parents, Ruth Feld, Rt. 4 Box 209, Watertown, WI 53094
A.L.L., P. O. Box 490, Stafford, VA 22554
Life and Liberty Letter, P. O. Box 1436, Southern Pines, NC 28387
Eagle Forum, Box 618, Alton, IL 62002

MORE FAITH-BUILDING BOOKS
BY HUNTINGTON HOUSE

MURDERED HEIRESS... LIVING WITNESS, by Dr. Petti Wagner, $5.95. This is the book of the year about Dr. Petti Wagner — heiress to a large fortune — who was kidnapped and murdered for her wealth, yet through a miracle of God lives today.

Dr. Wagner did indeed endure a horrible death experience, but through God's mercy, she had her life given back to her to serve Jesus and help suffering humanity.

Some of the events recorded in the book are terrifying. But the purpose is not to detail a violent murder conspiracy but to magnify the glorious intervention of God.

THE HIDDEN DANGERS OF THE RAINBOW: The New Age Movement and Our Coming Age of Barbarism, by Constance Cumbey, $5.95. A national best-seller, this book exposes the New Age Movement which is made up of tens of thousands of organizations throughout the world. The movement's goal is to set up a one-world order under the leadership of a false christ.

Mrs. Cumbey is a trial lawyer from Detroit, Mich., and has spent years exposing the New Age Movement and the false christ.

TRAINING FOR TRIUMPH: A Handbook for Mothers and Fathers, by Dr. W. George Selig and Deborah D. Cole, $5.95. Being a good mother and father is one of life's great challenges. However, most parents undertake that challenge with little or no preparation, according to Dr. Selig, a professor at CBN University. He says that often, after a child's early years are past, parents sigh: "Where did we go wrong?"

Dr. Selig, who has 20 years of experience in the field of education, carefully explains how to be good mothers and fathers and how to apply good principles and teachings while children are still young.

Feel Better and Live Longer Through: THE DIVINE CON-NECTION, by Dr. Donald Whitaker $4.95. This is a Christian's guide to life extension. Dr. Whitaker of Longview, Texas, says you really can feel better and live longer by following Biblical principles set forth in the word of God.

THE DIVINE CONNECTION shows you how to experience divine health, a happier life, relief from stress, a better appearance, a healthier outlook, a zest for living and a sound emotional life. And much, much more.

THE AGONY OF DECEPTION by Ron Rigsbee with Dorothy Bakker, $6.95. Ron Rigsbee was a man who through surgery became a woman and now through the grace of God is a man again. This book — written very tastefully — is the story of God's wonderful grace and His miraculous deliverance of a disoriented young man. It offers hope for millions of others trapped in the agony of deception.

THE DAY THEY PADLOCKED THE CHURCH, by H. Edward Rowe, $3.50. The warm yet heartbreaking story of Pastor Everett Sileven, a Nebraska Baptist pastor, who was jailed and his church padlocked because he refused to bow to Caesar. It is also the story of 1,000 Christians who stood with Pastor Sileven, in defying Nebraska tyranny in America's crisis of freedom.

BACKWARD MASKING UNMASKED Backward Satanic Messages of Rock and Roll Exposed, by Jacob Aranza, $4.95.
Are rock and roll stars using the technique of backward masking to implant their own religious and moral values into the minds of young people? Are these messages satanic, drug-related and filled with sexual immorality? Jacob Aranza answers these and other questions.

SCOPES II/THE GREAT DEBATE, by Louisiana State Senator Bill Keith, 193 pages, $4.95.
Senator Keith's book strikes a mortal blow at evolution

which is the cornerstone of the religion of secular humanism. He explains what parents and others can do to assure that creation science receives equal time in the school classrooms, where Christian children's faith is being destroyed.

WHY J.R.? A Psychiatrist Discusses the Villain of Dallas, by Dr. Lew Ryder, 152 pages, $4.95.

An eminent psychiatrist explains how the anti-Christian religion of Secular Humanism has taken over television programming and what Christians can do to fight back.

NEED A MIRACLE? by Harald Bredesen, 159 pages, $4.95

This book shows how to draw upon the greatest power in the universe to cope with "unsolvable" problems; "incurable" illnesses; enslaving habits; and day-to-day money shortages.

YES, LORD! by Harald Bredesen, 198 pages, $4.95.

This is a wonderful story of God's power and grace. Pat Boone said: "Knowing Harald Bredesen is a little like knowing Elijah. Miracles follow him wherever he goes."

218

YES, send me the following books:

_____ copy (copies) of **Globalism: America's Demise** @ $8.95 = _____

_____ copy (copies) of **Murdered Heiress . . . Living Witness** @ $5.95 = _____

_____ copy (copies) of **The Hidden Dangers of the Rainbow** @ $5.95 = _____

_____ copy (copies) of **The Divine Connection** @ $4.95 = _____

_____ copy (copies) of **The Agony of Deception** @ $6.95 = _____

_____ copy (copies) of **Training for Triumph** @ $4.95 = _____

_____ copy (copies) of **The Day They Padlocked The Church** @ $3.50 = _____

_____ copy (copies) of **Backward Masking Unmasked** @ $4.95 = _____

_____ copy (copies) of **Scopes II/The Great Debate** @ $4.95 = _____

_____ copy (copies) of **Why J.R.?** @ $4.95 = _____

_____ copy (copies) of **Need A Miracle?** @ $4.95 = _____

_____ copy (copies) of **Yes, Lord!** @ $4.95 = _____

Enclosed is: $ _____ including postage (please include $1 per book for postage) for _____ books.

Name _____

Address _____

City and State _____ Zip _____

Mail to Huntington House, Inc, P. O. Box 78205, Shreveport, Louisiana 71137

Telephone Orders: (TOLL FREE) 1-800-572-8213, or in Louisiana (318) 222-1350

Who Has The Children?
and
Where Are They Taking Them?

"EDUCATION FOR GLOBAL 2000" Lets Get A Handle On **Education!** *by William M. Bowen, Jr., Tape 1, #060, $5.95.*
A brief background in Humanism and how this philosophy is carried out in the education system today. Issues include *Guidance Counselors, Child Abuse and Neglect Laws, Death Education, Gifted and Talented, World Citizenship*, etc.

Declaration of Interdependence, Computers, MBO — Management by Objectives — Crisis Management, New Constitution – 1987, EST & ERA, Child Care/No Values, Liberation Theology, Change Agents.

"GLOBALISM & GLOBAL EDUCATION" Who's Who & Who's What? *by William M. Bowen, Jr., Tape 2, #061, $5.95.*
Specific timetable complete with foundations and other institutions orchestrating this *Global Plan.* (This is not a complete list by any means). Aspen Institute, 1930,

Rockefeller Foundation, Carnegie Foundation, John Dewey, 1933, National Education Association – NEA, United Nations, 1976, John Goodlad, 1987, Club of Rome, 1989, Jimmy Carter, City Bank.

"ZERO POPULATION" We've Got A Big Problem! (Covert & Overt) *by Bill & Penny Bowen, Tape 3, #062, $5.95.*

International Christian Media Radio Program, "Point of View" hosted by Marlin Maddoux. Interview Format Hi-Lighting *"Zero Population."* A major thrust in *ALL* public schools and some private schools. Eliminates Some 2.5 Billion People – HOW?, Abortion, Aids, Infanticide, Homosexuality, Suicide – Death Education, Euthanasia, Genocide.

"GLOBAL 2000 – PART 1" The Humanist Connection *by Bill & Penny Bowen, Tape 4, #063, $5.95.*

"Southwest Radio Church Program," hosted by David Webber. A direct hit on *All Major Issues* confronted by our children daily — including *Humanism – Globalism – New Age and Eastern Religions.*

"GLOBAL 2000 — PART 2" Deceit — Aimed at the Christians!, *by Bill & Penny Bowen, Tape 5, #064.*

New Age, New Values, New World Order, = Anti Christ?

Tape #4 & 5 come as a set. They can not be separated. $11.90

"A TANGLED WEB" How does it affect me?, *by William M. Bowen, Jr., Tape 6, #065, $5.95.*

An interview given before Robert Billings, the under secretary of education in Washington, D.C. August 1981. Includes "PROJECT BASIC" — A seven-state curriculum targeted for our nation.

"A NATION AT RISK" The Demise of America as We Know It, *By Bill & Penny Bowen, Tape 7, #066, $5.95.*

We are truly "A NATION AT RISK." Questions and answers to help you understand just what is going on today in the name of education.

Termination of parental rights, Federal Emergency Management Administration (FEMA), Comparative Religions, New Constitution, New Age — Demise of America as We Know It, Control — Chains on Kids.

"WHAT CAN I DO? — WE HAVE THE ANSWERS!" **Parents in Alliance for Academic Education,** *by Penny Bowen * H.E.R.O., Tape 8, #067, $5.95.*

Practical suggestions for you to act effectively in your own local area. These suggestions are for CHURCHES, TEACHERS, SCHOOLS, DADS AND MOMS. It includes HOUSEHOLD HINTS, POLITICAL ACTION ACTIVITIES AND FUNDRAISING, TELEPHONE TREES, NEWSLETTERS, Etc...

PRAYER + ACTION = RESULTS.

"SEMINAR DEALING WITH HUMANISM & GLOBAL EDUCATION" *by Bill & Penny Bowen, #069 VHS, 90 minute Video Cassette, $49.95.*

An account of how education is a vehicle for the ONE-WORLD ATHEISTIC GOVERNMENT.

Your children are being taught to accept WORLD CITIZENSHIP by DIVORCING them from their RELIGIOUS BELIEFS, their AMERICAN HERITAGE, and their PARENTS.

YES, send me the following tapes (circle numbers):

Tape 1, #060 "EDUCATING FOR GLOBAL 2000"		$5.95
Tape 2, #061 "GLOBALISM AND GLOBAL EDUCATION"		$5.95
Tape 3, #062 "ZERO POPULATION"		$5.95
Tape 4, #063		
Tape 5, #064 "GLOBAL 2000" — PART 1 & 2		$11.90
Tape 6, #065 "A TANGLED WEB"		$5.95
Tape 7, #066 "A NATION AT RISK"		$5.95

Tape 8, #067 "WHAT CAN I DO? WE HAVE
THE ANSWERS! $5.95

★★★★★★★

Complete 8-Tape Album "WHO HAS THE $39.95
#068-ALB   CHILDREN AND
WHERE ARE THEY
TAKING THEM?

★★★★★★★

VIDEO-VHS SEMINAR DEALING WITH $49.95
#069-VHS   HUMANISM AND GLOBAL
90 Minutes EDUCATION

Enclosed is: $_____ including postage
(please enclose $1 for postage and handling for first tape
and 50¢ for each additional tape) for _____ tapes.

Enclosed is: $_____ including postage
(please enclose $2 for postage and handling) for _____
90-MINUTE VIDEO/VHS.

NAME _____

ADDRESS _____

CITY _____

STATE _____ ZIP _____

Mail to Huntington House, Inc., P. O. Box 78205, Shreveport, LA 71137. Telephone Orders: (TOLL FREE) 1-800-
572-8213, or in Louisiana (318) 222-1350.